THE RENEWAL OF THE MIND

Mike Pratt

HODDER AND STOUGHTON
LONDON SYDNEY AUCKLAND TORONTO

British Library Cataloguing in Publication Data

Pratt, Mike
  The renewal of the mind. – (Hodder
  Christian Paperbacks).
  1. Spiritual life
  I. Title
  269   BV4501.2

ISBN 0 340 417781

THE RENEWAL OF
THE MIND

CONTENTS

INTRODUCTION

'Be transformed by the renewal of your mind'
(Rom. 12:2)

I want to take you on an unusual missionary journey. I invite you to come with me on the most important conversion work you will ever do. I want you to use this book to help you to see how the Lord Jesus can and will change your way of understanding everything so that you can become a more effective member of His Kingdom. The missionary expedition I invite you to make is into your own mind, to let it be transformed and renewed by Christ.

You might well ask why that is so important. I sincerely believe the renewal of our minds is the key factor towards the conversion of the Western world. The number of new Christians continues to increase rapidly in most parts of the world except in those dominated by European and North American cultures, but I am convinced the Lord desires to act in our culture as much as He is acting in others. However, for our part, we need to have a higher expectation that He will work among us, a high expectation generated from a right attitude of mind.

I offer this book to help create that right attitude.

What will that right attitude achieve?

It will open your eyes to discern God's activity in this world around us, in His creation and in people, as well as increasing your expectation in seeing Him work supernaturally. You will become someone who can recognise the Lord in all situations and seeing Him, will work with

Him in furthering His desire for the salvation of the world He loves. So as you read this book, you will find two sorts of story. There are stories from ordinary, everyday life, like marriage, schools, hospitals, and stories from meeting God 'supernaturally'. I offer *both* on an equal footing as learning experiences of having a renewed mind.

Yet, I shall have failed if after reading this book you have only learned some interesting ideas about renewing your mind. Of course, I hope you will use it for instruction, but my desire is that you will use it as a manual *and so discover for yourself*. Effective learning comes from what we do ourselves.

I therefore invite you to come on a missionary journey. Like all other missionary expeditions, you will expect *conversion*.

That will happen as we bring the Holy Spirit into our minds. Several chapters are therefore devoted to seeing how you can bring yourself before the Lord to ask Him to work renewal in your mind.

The initial chapters show how you can come to a clearer vision of the Lord and what that means for your life. These chapters discuss the familiar, traditional disciplines of dealing with sin, confession and repentance, not only for instruction, but to help you act on what is written and so begin the renewing process.

Only the Lord God has power to transform our minds, so we have to learn to come into His presence and wait on Him, asking Him to renew us. This book shows you how to use prayer, meditation, praise, Scripture and Holy Communion to wait expectantly on the Lord Jesus.

But missionary expeditions also include facing *difficulties*, and the renewal of our minds is no exception. The greatest difficulties most of us have in recognising the presence of God in both the natural and supernatural are our doubt and disbelief. These negative forces are so often the greatest obstacles we face, preventing the conversion of our way of thinking.

I shall show you how you can use these powerful

forces for good. I shall help you to use doubt and disbelief creatively, turning them into instruments for the renewal of your mind.

Naturally, I have written about my discoveries from my own journey, such as it is. They are my reflections on what I have seen and experienced, but I encourage and challenge you to discover all those things for yourself.

I offer you this book as an aid and partial guide on your missionary expedition to renewing your mind. I pray that as your mind becomes ever increasingly conformed to Christ's, He will use you mightily in bringing many of those near to you into His Kingdom.

1

THE BATTLE FOR THE MIND

Mind Formation

I remember one day my daughter, who was then about three years old, asking my wife, 'Mummy, did you eat Ben?'

Ben is her younger brother, and she had been told that Ben had come out of mummy's tummy, so how else except by eating could anything get into anyone's tummy, especially in the understanding of a three-year-old? Her developing mind was seeking an explanation of something of importance in ways it could understand at that stage of its formation.

Of course, to say what we all know, our minds are not given to us ready-made, they are formed and conditioned by the sort of experiences we receive over what are called our 'formative years'. In childhood, our developing mind responds in its own particular way, interpreting and relating to life around.

It seems to me that our minds exist to adapt us to the particular world in which we live. Perhaps even in babyhood our minds start absorbing information, discovering which experiences are good or bad, pleasurable or nasty, forming to help us live in our world. Our babies are surrounded by English-speakers. They absorb the language. Even from birth children 'begin' to take in those outside responses. Their minds form in relation to what they are receiving, so that long before they can talk fluently, they can understand what is being said to them.

But we also know children absorb attitudes. We do not need a degree in psychology to know that a child who is continually surrounded by criticism and rejection may well interpret that as meaning they are worthless and unlovable as people. Their minds have been formed to think of themselves in those sorts of terms. I can assure you, as can many others in the pastoral ministry, that when someone's mind has been formed like that over a long period of time, especially from childhood, it takes a mighty miracle to bring them to seeing themselves as worthy of love.

On the other hand, children who are surrounded by love and realistic praise of who they are, usually interpret their adult lives positively, because they normally have a high regard of themselves. Their minds have been formed to think in this way.

Of course, I know that there is far more to bringing up children well than the quality of their immediate family life. This part of the chapter is not about child-rearing, but about sharing how past experiences can and do shape how we see ourselves and our world – if you like, what sort of spectacles we wear.

Yet all of us, and perhaps especially our children, absorb other things from our environment which condition how our minds respond to life. One of the struggles we have had to face in our family has been the result of moving some years ago from a relatively poor area in England to a prosperous London suburb. The struggle is the pressure of 'materialism'. In the poorer area, because there was little money, the people seemed not to bother much with material prosperity. They adapted to life in that environment; but in the richer suburb, personal self-worth seems to be identified with size of house, number of cars, and the amount of money being earned. I am not saying that is either good or bad, but we have noticed that we have started thinking in 'materialistic' ways. We were not even aware that we had been taking on the area's values. They seemed to creep up on us and become part of us simply by our living in the area.

Values, attitudes and concerns are learnt from those around us, forming and shaping our minds. But there is also something to add which is of fundamental importance. Everyone, and every family, is surrounded and immersed in what the nation as a whole values and believes. These values are spread through the schools, the media, and all the structures of society. They permeate our minds. Such beliefs and values may not be written up, but they are in the air we all breathe. If you are English, you will be immersed in the prevailing values and beliefs of England. Those things filter through the media, the law, education, and through the people we meet. The prevailing values will be everywhere. Even when foreigners settle in other countries, though they may try to preserve their old ways of life, their children will still absorb the prevailing beliefs of their new country.

Yet it is not just that we are immersed in the values and beliefs of where we live, but that those things help form how we think and respond to the world around us. They shape our minds, and consequently condition how we think about ourselves and the world.

The Battle for the Mind

Not so long ago, I heard this challenge from someone who is a leading exponent on Church growth.

There are more born-again Christians in Africa than nominal Christians in the whole of Europe! The Church in Africa is growing faster there than the birth-rate. The dead are being raised in Indonesia.

'Why is it,' asks the missionary, 'miracles happen overseas, but not in this country? After all, God is the same, the healer is the same, what or who is different?'

Most Western Christians have heard comments such
as these, and have, I hope, been challenged by them.
What has happened for the Church in this country to
have lost its impetus? Why is it that perhaps less than 10
per cent of the population in the United Kingdom will
attend a place of worship next Sunday? Why is it that
significant numbers of church-goers, even 'born-again
Christians', find it difficult to believe that God will
give miraculous signs, including healing, in our own
churches?

I believe it is because we are children of a secular
culture. Secularism is a word which means that we
understand and respond to life, all of life, without
bothering to refer to God at all.

Science taught it to us. Perhaps that was behind the
conflict between Charles Darwin and those who held the
truth of the story of Adam and Eve. Darwin offered a
'natural' explanation of man's beginnings, whereas
Genesis declares we cannot understand our origins without reference to God. Yet in more ways than one, the
battle was lost by those who believed in those Biblical
stories, because that so-called scientific attitude has
spread to every dimension of life in our sort of society.
*The prevailing attitude we all absorb is one that understands
and responds to life as if there was no God.* Consequently,
ethics, or how we behave, are not thought of as breaking
God's law, but as more to do with giving us what we
want. Abortions are not murders, but inconveniences,
homosexuality is considered an acceptable natural state,
accumulation of personal wealth is a sign of success, and
so on. Our society does not think about its accountability
to God. It functions as if He did not exist.

We who live in this Western scientific society soak
in those same forces which shape those attitudes and
consequently block our ability to see God at work.

For example, some time ago I was used to bring healing
to a woman who had curvature of the spine. She had
undergone several operations, but she continued to

deteriorate. She was not a member of my church, but after prayer she was discovered in the ladies' cloakroom dressed only in her bra and pants, doing handsprings, somersaults, and backward bends!

'Look, look!' she declared to all who came in. 'I am healed! Look, here are the scars on my back from all my operations. The Lord has healed me! Praise His name!'

Naturally, I did not see any of those antics in the cloakroom, but one of the women in my church told me all about it. Yet someone standing nearby said: 'Isn't it marvellous what power the mind can have over the body!'

In New Testament times when most people saw Jesus's miracles they gave glory to God; God was an integral part of the way they understood their world. Yet here, before his own eyes, our twentieth-century Westerner sees a marvel, but can only understand it with a mind formed by our society's prevalent attitude!

Spiritual Dangers

That is serious enough. But there is something even more serious. St Paul puts it like this: 'the god of this world *has blinded the minds* of the unbelievers *to keep them from seeing* the light of the gospel of the glory of Christ' (2 Cor. 4:4; my italics).

It is not just that we no longer have the capacity to respond to the presence of God around us. Incapacity is one thing, but Paul declares that these mind-forming forces and powers prevent us, even imprison us, from seeing anything different. Have you ever overheard two people with opposing views on politics arguing? They never really see what the other is talking about, because their minds exclude information which does not fit in with how they expect things to be.

I think the Pharisees and the High Priests must have had great difficulty with the Lord Jesus and His teachings precisely because their minds were already fixed on how they thought God related to His world. They thought they knew how God treated sinners; He would punish them and cast them out. So that is what they did to sinners in their society, they made them outcasts. But the Lord Jesus came along and offered these outcasts God's forgiveness and became friends with them. No wonder the Lord disturbed the religious authorities! His mind did not work like theirs.

The Pharisees thought they knew how the Messiah, the Christ, would come. 'But as for this man [Jesus] we do not know where He comes from' (John 9:29). Trouble was brewing. The way their minds worked blocked them from seeing God's truth in Jesus.

And as if all that blindness in seeing God at work was not enough, it became even more serious. Rather than examining their perceptions, the Pharisees and High Priests handed Jesus over to Pilate as a heretic and blasphemer. Minds which are set away from God are not only blind to recognising Him at work, but they also *reject* Him and *deny* Him the right to do His works.

Even the Lord Jesus could do no mighty works in His home-town because of their disbelief. You can imagine what His neighbours said. 'Who, him? That little boy who used to run to the shop for me? The one who used to help old Joseph the carpenter? Are you telling me that *he* is performing miracles? Come off it. I've known his family and him for years, and they don't go in for things like that!' They do not believe in Him because their minds are already made up. They have their preconceptions of who Jesus is, but those views *prevent* the Lord from working in their midst. Who knows how many distressed persons did not receive healing because their minds were already set in such a way as to refuse the new-style Jesus.

This is a hard message to grasp. It was said quite cynically some years ago that miracles happen when people believe miracles will happen. (What the speaker meant, of course, was that miracles didn't really happen, but religious people will always 'think' they have.) Perhaps the truth of the matter is rather the reverse, that God does *not work* when people's minds are set against Him. Jesus certainly refused to produce miracles to satisfy His unbelieving critics. He did not come down from the cross as the priests mockingly told Him to do. Their disbelief blocked them from seeing God in Jesus and led them to the conviction that He, the Lord of all, must be executed.

It would be quite wrong to think of the religious authorities of Jesus's time as being morally corrupt and wicked people. I have no doubt that they rejected and crucified the Lord in full sincerity that they were doing God's will. After all, Jesus had broken the Sabbath, as they understood it, by healing the sick. There was a story circulating that Jesus had threatened to destroy the temple, God's own house, and build another within three days. They acted to preserve what they believed their God had given them, but they had got it wrong. Religious ritual, laws and practices and even good moral living are not in themselves evidence that someone is properly mindful of God. In fact, as the tragedy of Jesus's death demonstrates, even a sincerely held belief in God can blind its adherents and cause them to reject Him.

Even the Laws of Moses can forge a frame of mind which can miss God!

Perhaps that's one of the anxieties Paul had for the church he started in Galatia. He writes: 'Does he who supplies the Spirit to you and works miracles among you do so by works of the law, or by hearing with faith?' (Gal. 3:5). Possibly, he who describes himself as 'advanced in Judaism beyond many of my own age among my people, so extremely zealous was I for the traditions of my fathers' (1:14) knew more than most that minds formed around the Laws of Moses alone could be blind to recognising when God is at work. After all, he had supervised the execution of Stephen. No wonder he was angry that the Galatians had turned back 'to the weak and beggarly elemental spirits whose slaves you want to be? You observe days, and months, and seasons, and years! I am afraid I have laboured over you in vain' (4:9–11).

Paul is not referring to demonic activity when he talks about weak elemental spirits, rather he means the forces and powers which control us. It seems he meant their desire to take on Jewish laws!

He knows that if they do so they will become blind to God and reject His purpose for them and for the Gentile world.

So what is the nub of the challenge to Western Christians? Why is it that we do not experience the Lord moving mightily in our midst? I should like to suggest that it is because we have imbibed the milk of secularism from our host culture. Secularism is today's weak and beggarly elemental spirit which brings us bondage. We didn't drink that milk consciously. Thinking and responding to life as if there was no God simply soak into us from our environment. Secularism permeates our schools, colleges and churches and has infiltrated the Christian mind. So extensive is its influence in the Church that it is now taken almost for granted by some theologians that Jesus did not perform miracles; they doubt the truth of the Virgin Birth; they question the reality of the empty tomb, disbelieving that Jesus actually rose from the dead. And how do they justify their doubts? They say these stories were invented by religious people to convince others (who naturally expected God to be able to do those things) that God was really present in Jesus. I maintain that such theologians, sincere as they are, are blind to seeing God at work, because their minds have been formed by the forces of this world.

Yet I do not want in the slightest to suggest that such blindness to the so-called supernatural in the New Testament is *the* problem which we must solve to have renewed minds. It is rather a symptom of an all-embracing outlook on life which is fundamentally flawed. All of us are products of our Western secular culture and though its mind-forming forces may not have blocked some of us from recognising the hand of God in what we call the miraculous, we may have been blinded to seeing Him at work within everything else in His creation, in the ordinary and the natural, and *that* is the true test of whether or not we see and know God clearly. It is worth asking ourselves if we really do have the mind of Christ. When we look at Jesus's ministry, we certainly see that His work abounded with miracles and healing. He had a supernatural ministry and His opponents were blind to it. However, the Lord had a profound natural ministry too! He could see His Father within everything that was around Him. Continually, He invited His followers to look at the lilies of the field, to observe the farmer scattering his seed, to notice the housewife as she kneaded her bread mix or searched for a lost coin. These things too, for Jesus, proclaimed God and His Kingdom. He could see His Father there, within the midst of the ordinary.

Over and over again the Lord introduced His parables with this phrase 'The Kingdom of heaven is as . . .' He saw and noticed things of God because His mind was formed differently from those around. He saw life through God-fashioned perceptions. And what's more, He expected His followers to do the same, because so often at the end of His stories, Jesus challenged His hearers, 'He who has ears, let him hear', demanding whether they too could discern how God speaks through the ordinary things of life.

Now that presents us with a challenge, too. Do we not breed that strangest of all creatures – the secular Christian someone who expects to meet God in church on Sundays, but is blind to His working in ordinary, daily life, someone who wants to see the Lord answer prayer in a prayer-meeting, but has no conception that the answer was given at last week's trade-union meeting? The secular Christian who might have 'two minds', if such a thing were possible – one for religious use, and the other for ordinary, secular use. The challenge to Western Christians is not how we can take a leap of faith and embrace the miraculous and supernatural, adding that on to how we normally relate to life. The challenge is how we can have a radically different way of understanding and relating to the world which has been fashioned and formed by God, so that we can work with Him in His world both 'naturally and supernaturally'.

Our secularism has deceived us and blinded us.

We must ask ourselves those questions which challenged me. 'Why doesn't the Lord move as mightily in our lives as He does in people of *other cultures*?'

I should like to suggest that the way we think about and perceive God, the world, the Church and ourselves, the way we respond and act, our very minds have been corrupted by secularism. We do not expect God to be around. Consequently, our minds are blinded by the god of this world and we are in gross danger of rejecting Him even when He is before our faces. The major challenge for us is who shall have our minds. For too long we have been 'conformed to this world' (Rom. 12:2), 'conformed to the passions of your former ignorance' (1 Pet. 1:14), loving 'the things in the world' (1 John 2:15). The battle is not new, every Christian generation has to face it. It is the battle for the mind.

2

SETTING OUR MINDS

'Set your minds on things that are above' (Col. 3:2)

When I was a teenager, I set my mind on being a scientist.
I was going to go to university, study science and gain a
doctorate. It was a vision which fired me, and changed
my whole direction of life. For Christmas and birthday presents I asked for science text-books. Most of
them were far too old for me, and as a teenager I never
really understood them, but I still read them as if I
did. I spent hours and hours over many years poring
over those books because I was set on what I was
going to be. I had a large chemistry set in the spare bed-
room, and I went to scientific conferences. I was really
keen, so I worked and studied hard to pass my examina-
tions to go to university and study science. I am not
unique in being like that! When your mind is made up
to be something or do something, your whole life
becomes geared to achieving what your mind is set
on.

Our minds *need something* to respond to. They need a
focus, a goal, a vision. They always work well when they
are fixed on something. If they do not know 'what the
things above' are, they cannot be set on them, so they will
simply be set on the things of this world, and we have
seen in the previous chapter how minds formed by this
world blind us to recognising the Lord God. And that is
very dangerous, after all, 'To set the mind on the flesh is

death . . . the mind that is set on the flesh is hostile to God' (Rom. 8:6–7).

If we want our minds to be renewed, if we are prepared to enter the battle to stop them being conformed by the pressures and values of this world, then we must first 'set our minds on the things of the Spirit' (v. 5).

Here is a story to illustrate the point.

It was a warm, sunny afternoon. I cannot remember what I was doing, but soon I was to be put into a moving situation which would form one of the most important events in my life.

I was fairly young in the ministry, and I think most of my knowledge had at that time been gleaned from study at college, and had to be tested and grounded in what people call 'real life'.

My boss, who was also the chaplain to the local hospital, was away, and had asked me to give emergency cover for the hospital in case someone desperately wanted to see a clergyman. It had happened before, and usually nothing particular occurred. This day was going to be very different.

The telephone rang, and I picked it up. 'Mike Pratt here.'

'Oh, Mr Pratt,' said a woman's voice, 'I am the Sister in charge of the Coronary Care Unit in the hospital. We have just admitted a minister who has had a massive heart attack. He is very ill, and his wife has asked that he be anointed. Could you come as soon as possible, please?'

My boss had told me about anointing. It is a ceremony of praying for healing for the sick, and finds its Biblical authority in the Letter of James.

So as quickly as possible I went down to the church, picked up the olive-oil used for the service and dashed up to the Unit.

To say the least, it is rather distressing to see someone in a Coronary Care Unit. This poor man was stripped bare except for a modesty cloth; there seemed to be wires attached to him everywhere; he was surrounded by all sorts of measuring machines; and over his face was an oxygen mask. I remember it was very hot that afternoon. He was seriously ill, and he was unconscious. What an awful, dreadful state to be in!

I found his wife. She told me he was called Peter. And after spending a little time talking with her and, I hope, giving some comfort, I anointed him, asking the Holy Spirit to forgive him his sins and to come with His healing power.

Three hours later I returned to the ward to see how he was. I went first into the Unit office.

'How is Peter, Sister?'

'Not at all well, Mike,' she replied. 'Since you came in, he has had several other minor heart attacks. I am afraid he hasn't much longer. However, he has gained consciousness. He came round just after you left.'

I left the office and walked over to where Peter was lying. All the wires and contraptions were still there, and that oxygen mask. His wife was standing behind him, and his head in his oxygen mask was turned away from me.

I asked gently, 'How are you feeling, Peter?'

His head turned slowly towards me and through the mask I saw the most marvellous of smiles. He looked up at me and simply proclaimed, 'Glory be to God on high!'

My eyes filled! Here on his death-bed, strapped down with the trappings of modern medicine, this saint was rejoicing! He radiated joy.

I cannot remember how the next stage happened, but I was outside the ward talking with Peter's wife. (We were both brimful of tears by then.)

'Did you know,' she said to me, 'it is Peter's birthday today?'

She wiped back a tear, and continued, 'Do you know the first thing he said to me when he recovered consciousness? He said, "Darling, isn't it wonderful, I am going to receive the fullness of my salvation on my birthday.'''

He died later that night. This wasn't the usual sort of miracle, it was something far more important. It was the story of one man, an ordinary man, who knew the reality of God's promises for himself. This was true not only in the sense that he knew what the Scriptures say, rather he knew what they said and had grasped them, *making the promises his own. His mind, and so his thinking and understanding and living and dying in this world, was shaped by the hope to come.* He had, to use another phrase from St Paul, set his mind 'on things that are above', where Christ is (Col. 3:1–2), and his response to his death had been *formed* by that God-promised future.

Peter demonstrated for me a profound spiritual truth – the truth that when anyone sets their mind on the Lord, they enter into a two-way relationship. *Seeing Him and the things above, those self-same objects and Person on which our minds are set, begin to change US and alter the way we see and understand ourselves and the world around.*

St Paul wrote 'And we all, with unveiled face, *beholding the glory of the Lord, are being changed* into his likeness from one degree of glory to another; for this comes from the Lord who is the Spirit' (2 Cor. 3:18; my italics).

The Transforming Presence

First of all, *what* had Peter grasped?
   It was something like this:

Then I saw a new heaven and a new earth . . . and I heard a loud voice from the throne saying, 'Behold, the dwelling of God is with men. He will dwell with them, and they shall be his people, and God himself will be with them; he will wipe away every tear from their eyes, and death shall be no more, neither shall there be mourning nor crying nor pain any more, for the former things have passed away.' And he who sat upon the throne said, 'Behold, I make all things new' (Rev. 21:1–5).

I wonder which of those promises you think were the ones which made Peter so joyful. No more death? No more pain? I do not think so. I believe it was *the* promise which is the basis of all the other things happening. It is the promise that *God himself will be with us*. That is what fired Peter. This is what St Paul wrote to the Philippians, 'My desire is to depart and be with Christ' (1:23). Paul did not even write about receiving the blessings of no more persecutions, no more problems with troublesome churches, no more problems with his health, his desire was simply to be with Christ. So when the Thessalonians need comfort over their grief for loved ones who have died, he writes, 'we shall always be with the Lord. Therefore comfort one another with these words' (1 Thess. 4:17–18). The promise is that He will dwell with us, and we shall be with Him. Of course that sounds wonderful, but I think we need to know a little more before we can understand why Peter was full of joy when he knew he was going to be with the Lord.

This story might help.

I may be gifted in some areas of life, but unfortunately in one area, I confess I am not. My weakness is not being able to teach religion in English state schools to 15-16-year-old young adults. In some countries this could never happen, but it happens in the UK by law, if not in reality. I was asked to teach groups for about an hour. Well, I thought it was an interesting programme. I thought it gave plenty of scope for fruitful discussion and contribution. What it was I do not know, but what I had on my hands was a sort of apathetic blackboard jungle. The class was not violent or nasty, it was simply unco-operative. They turned their backs, they chatted together. It was chaos, and they did nothing despite my efforts and protests.

Until one afternoon. Ever so quietly, the headmaster slipped into the back of the classroom. Of course, they all had noticed him there; I, too, noticed him there. He did not say a word. He did not move a finger, but he was *very* present. That half-hour was the best teaching I have ever done! I was 'inspired' to reach new heights of enthusiasm. And my students? A miracle happened. I have never been with such a co-operative group – they discussed, challenged, innovated . . . they brought joy to any teacher's heart, especially to mine. My normal hell had been turned into heaven. Why? Because the head-teacher was there. He transformed my class.

What were my lessons? For a start, the whole *feel* of the class changed. Quite suddenly, there was an air of expectation, even excitement, as the students became alert, waiting to seize their opportunity of contributing to the world of learning and self-discovery. Not only were they attentive, but they were even sitting on the edge of their seats, their hands shooting up into the air as they vied with each other to catch my attention so they could advance the course of their academic prowess. The atmosphere was electric and stimulating. It felt marvellous! It's the sort of *feel* I suppose good teachers always have with their students, even if they are teaching religious knowledge. By being there, the headmaster had created expectation and eagerness to learn in all present.

I asked myself what it must feel like when we are aware of God's presence with us. What does He create in His world simply because He is there?

The feeling is *joy*. Indeed, when God is actually present, joy fills the whole universe.

Say among the nations, 'The Lord reigns!
Yea, the world is established, it shall never be moved;
he will judge the peoples with equity.'
Let the heavens be glad, and let *the earth rejoice*;
let the sea roar, and all that fills it;
let the field exult, and everything in it!

Then shall all the *trees of the wood sing for joy*
before the LORD, for he comes, for he comes to
judge the earth (Ps. 96:10–13; my italics).

We can recognise the same feeling of joy in people's
hearts in this picture of heaven

Then I heard what seemed to be the voice of a great
multitude, like the sound of many waters and like the
sound of mighty thunderpeals, crying, 'Hallelujah'.
For *the Lord* our God the Almighty *reigns*. Let us *rejoice*
and *exult* and give him the glory, for the marriage of the
Lamb has come, and his Bride has made herself ready'
(Rev. 19:6–7; my italics).

But joy is there because the Lord God is present. *His
presence makes it happen*. It is how He changes those
who are aware of His presence. So, I hope, we now
have a deeper understanding of why Peter was filled
with joy. It was the sure sign that the Lord Himself
was with him, creating that joy in his heart, mind and
soul.

Peter was truly set on the things above, but those same
things transformed his death-bed from a place of sorrow
to one of rejoicing. He declared, 'Glory be to God on
high.'

But what did Peter mean when he said, 'Isn't it
wonderful, I shall receive my full salvation on my birthday'?

The headmaster taught me another lesson. There were
benefits of his being there. For once the class actually did
something creative and educational. We operated in the
way the headteacher expected his school to operate.
When I saw how it applies when God is present in His
creation, wonderful and marvellous things started to
dawn on me. This is how it will be, simply because God is
there in the midst.

There shall be NO MORE:
>   Death
>   Mourning
>   Pain
>   Evil
>   Sin (Rev. 21:1–8).

There shall be:
>   Worship
>   Life
>   Healing
>   Peace (Rev. 21:22–22:5).

God's presence conveys wholeness, salvation and health to the whole people.

That is how it will be when the Lord God reigns over His creation and over His people. So no wonder men and women like St Paul and Peter strain forward to what lies ahead, pressing on towards the goal of the upward call of God. They have not only grasped the vision, but have been grasped by it. Their minds are set on being with the Lord, but they also see what He will do for them and for the world, and seeing it, their minds are formed by it, and their lives directed to living and dying for it.

Setting our minds on the Lord Jesus

I suppose it would be quite reasonable for someone who was not a Christian to accuse us of pursuing 'pie in the sky', wondering what good all those hopes of heaven have for this world and this life. Is all that Peter showed us so heavenly-minded that it is of no earthly use? Do we, as some of our critics suggest, delude ourselves in our religion by pursuing future dreams to escape the harsh realities of this world?

Now, I am sure we share with Jewish people a belief in those future promises of God, but there is also something special and unique about the Christian faith. We believe

Jesus Christ was sent from God to bring something of those promises here and now into this world. Jesus's ministry shows us two things – what our future with God will be like when the Kingdom of God comes at the end of the world; and the good news that God's rule has now entered into our world and has started to give us a taste of what one day will be. In other words, although Christians look to being with the Lord in the future, they know the Lord has come and comes now into this world and has already begun to change it.

When my children were smaller, being typically noisy, they were seldom invited to wedding receptions. One of the advantages of clerical life is that our house is right next-door to where wedding receptions take place, so in those days it was easy to slip home and see how the children were. When we popped in, they always asked one question: 'What's the wedding like?'

We did, of course, try and explain all the delightful foods and delicacies we had eaten, and we tried to tell them what sort of wedding it was – happy, dull, lots of laughter and so on. But what they were really waiting for was that moment when my wife would open her bag and produce some of that lovely food. Our children soon worked out what sort of wedding reception we were attending! They sampled it. They had a taste of it and in a small part had become involved in it.

So when we look at Jesus's ministry, we should catch a glimpse of what it is like when God is with all His creation. We believe the Lord has brought something of God's Kingdom to earth and thereby involved us all in it, by letting us taste it. Since God's presence is characterised by joy, wholeness, and power transforming those whose minds are set on Him, we should recognise those three things in Jesus's ministry.

Read the Gospel stories and notice how those around the Lord Jesus must have been overjoyed at seeing their blind friends see, their lame children walking. Imagine yourself to be the widow of Nain on the way to bury your only son. How would you feel when Jesus raised your dead child back to life? God was there. Jesus is Emmanuel (which means God-with-us).

Besides joy, we can obviously recognise the benefits of God's presence through the Lord Jesus; the dead were raised, the sick healed, the disruptive creation stilled, the sinner reconciled. All that is quite plain to see, but what is especially important was His impact on those around Him. When we look at Jesus's ministry in the Gospels, we see a transforming presence working in all who put their trust in Him, shaping the whole outlook of those whose minds were made up that He was the Messiah. In other words, Jesus changed those whose minds were set on Him. St John wrote, 'And the Word became flesh and dwelt among us, full of grace and truth; we have beheld His glory, glory as of the only Son from the Father' (John 1:14).

But not only did they behold, through such setting of their minds they also *'from His fulness . . . received, grace upon grace'* (v. 16; my italics).

Being with Jesus, set on Him, changed them. He transformed a group of semi-literate, half-educated, small-minded men into a dynamic, love-packed apostleship with confidence to go to the four corners of the known world with a message validated because it was lived out to the full. Their total outlook on life had been changed.

How? St Luke records in Acts 4:13: 'Now when they (the Jewish authorities) saw the boldness of Peter and John, and perceived that they were uneducated, common men, they wondered; and they recognised that *they had been with Jesus*' (my italics). Jesus's disciples had been changed because they had eyes only for Him. They followed Him, they sought Him out, they were with Him, and being set on Him, He transformed them and their whole way of understanding and relating to the world. They had been given something of the mind of Christ.

But what is especially exciting is that the Lord did not only change them to think about God's world as He did, He also transformed them so they could act in this world as He did. The disciples not only witnessed healing signs at the hand of Jesus, but *became themselves* channels of God's healing to others. They received His love, and then *became givers of it*. Indeed the genuine test of having been with Jesus was to 'love one another as I have loved you' (John 15:12).

The changed became the changers. They gave what they had received and altered the course of human history.

Finally, both Peter on his death-bed and Jesus's first disciples teach us something which we must all do if we want the Lord to change and renew the way we see and relate to His world; we must set our minds on the Lord Jesus and the things above. He has power to change us when we are centred on Him, and being transformed, we too shall bring joy and wholeness into this world.

The next chapter describes what happens as we begin to focus clearly on the Lord.

3

FOCUSING ON THE LORD

Do you know anything about photography? My camera is quite old-fashioned compared with modern ones because I still have to twiddle and turn dials and rings to focus on my subjects. However, I know that the more sensitively I can focus, the better the photograph.

Taking photographs is helpful in understanding a little more about setting our minds on the Lord. If we look to Him in some sort of general, unspecific way, but never actually asking His direction in our life, then, not surprisingly, His impact on our lives will be quite fuzzy and not very discernible, just like an out-of-focus photograph. However, if we focus clearly on the Lord, then we shall see quite definitely how He is changing and renewing the way we respond to life.

Expert photographers can teach us how to take well-defined photographs, and similarly various people in the Bible can teach us how to get a clear picture of God. Isaiah is one example. His experience recorded in Isaiah 6:1–7 describes what happens when we have our first true sight of the Lord and how we can become focused on Him.

The prophet writes:

In the year that King Uzziah died I saw the Lord sitting upon a throne, high and lifted up; and his train filled the temple. Above him stood the seraphim; each had six wings: with two he covered his face, and with two he covered his feet, and with two he flew. And one called to another and said:

'Holy, holy, holy is the Lord of hosts;
the whole earth is full of his glory.'

And the foundations of the thresholds shook at the voice of him who called, and the house was filled with smoke. And I said: 'Woe is me! For I am lost; for I am a man of unclean lips, and I dwell in the midst of a people of unclean lips; for my eyes have seen the King, the Lord of hosts!'

Then flew one of the seraphim to me, having in his hand a burning coal which he had taken with tongs from the altar. And he touched my mouth, and said: 'Behold, this has touched your lips; your guilt is taken away, and your sin forgiven.'

The first lesson. Isaiah saw the Lord, but the lesson is in the impact the vision had upon him. *Isaiah became deeply conscious of the true nature of the person of God and the relationship between God and man.* He saw that God is great, majestic and glorious, and mankind is small and insignificant. He saw the Lord enthroned as King and recognised that we were little more than dust of the earth. Isaiah experienced the right perspective we should all have in our relationship with the Lord, and he also captured the proper feelings of awe, wonder, fear and insignificance. He teaches us that this is what truly happens when anyone sees the Lord: we respond to the fact that He is God, the Holy One, the Creator of the whole universe. He is LORD! Job, too, saw God. Right at the end of the Book of Job, God speaks to him and reveals Himself. Forgetting God had not answered his questions about innocent suffering, Job declared: 'I had heard of thee by the hearing of the ear, but now my eye sees thee; therefore I despise myself, and repent in dust and ashes' (Job 42:5–6).

The second lesson we learn from Isaiah's vision is that he was convicted of his own sin and the sinfulness of the people (compare the above passage from Job). It is almost as if a camera has been pointed at a very bright light, and its aperture has to close automatically to prevent that brightness destroying its film.

The truth is that no one can have a clear picture of God without becoming overwhelmingly aware of his/her sin and sinfulness. In the first instance, such awareness of our sin can make us want to shut out the glory of God. Perhaps that is what happened to St Peter when the Lord Jesus ordered him to put down his nets for the great catch of fish. 'Depart from me, for I am a sinful man, O Lord' (Luke 5:8).

That is what happened to Paul on the Damascus road. He saw the glory of the risen Lord, that light far brighter than the noonday sun, and he was blinded (Acts 9:1–8). Perhaps the loss of his sight symbolised an initial spiritual reaction as his mind and soul closed over under the glaring light of Jesus the Lord. No doubt he, too, became very aware of his sin.

The third lesson Isaiah shows is that no one can continue gazing at the Lord God unless their sin is dealt with. True focusing on God therefore demands that we must be cleansed from our sins as Isaiah was from his.

Indeed, the New Testament is consistent in its teaching that no one can enter God's presence unless they have been cleansed of all their sin. We look with longing to that time when God will dwell with us, but it is preceded by the Day of Judgment when the Lord Christ will root out all causes of sin and evil-doers from His Kingdom. Even if we prefer to set our minds on the ascended Lord Jesus, we must recognise that before He entered the joy of Resurrection life, He went through the agony of Good Friday. On that day, God declared His judgment on sin.

Sin is serious, so serious that it was the cause of the Lord Jesus's death. No one will ever enter God's presence unless they have been cleansed of all their sin.

Jesus told a parable to underline that most fundamental of all truths. It is recorded in Matthew 22:1–14.

On the face of it, the story seems very unjust. The king wanted his marriage feast to be filled with lots of people. The invited guests all made their excuses as to why they could not come, so the king ordered his servants to go out into the streets and invite everybody in, both good and bad. That seems extremely generous, but then there is a sting in the tail. The king came in to look at the guests and saw a man who was not dressed in a wedding outfit, and had him thrown out. How unfair! Or so it seems to us who go to weddings already dressed for the occasion. But they did not do it like that in Jesus's time. The king would have *provided* his guests with their wedding outfits when they arrived. This man had presumably not bothered to put his on, and thereby had treated his host with contempt. If our desire is to be with the Lord, let us be rid of our sin. He has provided the means to wash our sins away.

Isaiah's vision teaches us about the rightful recognition of the lordship of God over everything. He teaches us about the seriousness of our sinful nature and the necessity to be cleansed from our sins. He teaches us what it is to be focused on the Lord.

The Lord Jesus can start transforming and renewing our minds when we have set ourselves on a *clear* picture of who He is and who we are, so we have to begin the focusing procedure. We have to learn and apply what Isaiah has shown us, not just when we were converted, but all of the time, and the New Testament shows us how to focus on the Lord through what it calls 'confession'.

First of all, let me explain what 'confession' means.

A Sort of Confession

What a way! Eating horribly cold chicken-legs for a hastily-prepared picnic in the front seat of a small cramped car, overlooking the miserable early-spring bare wastes of Windsor Great Park on a cold, damp, drizzling day, I declared my love for Frances – the girl at my side – and asked her to marry me!

There was no room for romance. Never mind getting down on to one knee, there was no room in that car even to cross your legs, and who wanted to get pneumonia out there in that Thames-side mist!

But Frances (after choking on her chicken-leg – I rather took her by surprise) seemed not to notice the conditions surrounding my declaration of love. Romantic notions seemed to go out of the car-window into the afternoon's greyness, for she simply heard nothing but my confession of love. It seemed to me that all her senses focused on to what she had heard.

The reason why I have told you about that very precious moment in our lives is not to make you glad to hear that she responded by saying 'yes', but rather to tell you the obvious truth that not many people do get married unless they, in one definite way or other, confess their love to the one they want to marry. 'It's all very well, mother,' the heartbroken young woman sobs, in the teenage romance stories, 'John acts as if he loves me, but he has never told me that he does.' She knows nothing is likely to happen until he declares his love.

But the truth is that *declaration of love changes things*. The relationship between the man and the woman changes. Even if there is refusal, it can never be the same between them because definite positions have been openly declared and will have to be accepted or rejected. The relationship will enter into a creative phase leading into marriage, or tension and anxiety leading to possible breakdown if the proposal is rejected. One thing is sure, life will never be the same again, and that is why, of course, we think and pray very seriously before confessing our love and declaring our intention.

Such *speaking out* from the heart, such telling forth of our deepest being, with all the implications of relationships being changed is what the Scriptures mean by *confession*.

'Confession' is used in two important ways in the New Testament, but in whatever way the word is used it always carries the meaning *to declare openly* what our heart feels or knows, in the realisation that by so doing *relationships between ourselves, God and others* will be fundamentally changed.

Applying Isaiah's First Lesson: Confessing Jesus as Lord

St Paul writes in his letter to the Romans, 'if you *confess* with your lips that Jesus is Lord and believe in your heart that God raised him from the dead, you will be saved. For man believes with his heart and so is justified, and he *confesses* with his lips and so is saved' (Rom. 10:9–10; my italics).

Confessing Jesus is Lord is, of course, far more serious than any heartfelt declaration of love between a man and a woman, but similarly includes both *declaring openly* what we feel or know about Jesus, in the realisation that by so doing, *the relationship between Him and ourselves will be fundamentally changed*. Confession then not only states who we know Jesus is, but becomes the means of changing our relationship with Him. As once the lover confesses his or her love for the beloved and their relationship can no longer remain as it was, so, too, confession of Jesus as our Lord, if truly declared, becomes the means of making Him Lord in our lives. However, we must make a true confession, and, like any other declaration, it needs to be done openly. *Confession must be open.*

I am always suspicious of those who say they are Christians, but find it too embarrassing to state quietly that Jesus is the Lord. Simply speaking 'Jesus, you are Lord', out loud, declares the position in which we stand with Him.

When I was a boy there used to be gang fights in our

local woods, and the two gangs involved used to recruit for the evening battle in the school playground. We 'neutral' boys would suddenly be surrounded by the opposing gangs who would then start to persuade us to join their side. You had to decide for one or the other, or you would be beaten up by both gangs! You could not be neutral. But when you moved to one gang, you obviously identified with them. They were your allies, the others were your opponents. The boundaries were drawn. When we openly declare 'Jesus is Lord', we declare our position, *first of all to ourselves*. Jesus is with whom I identify. He is my Lord. *It is a declaration to myself that He who has charge over my life*. Jesus now gives the orders, and has authority in my life. I find it a very useful simple prayer that when things are going wrong in my life to shout out (somewhere discreet) 'Jesus you are my Lord.' It has a remarkable effect of bringing my life back into order. Such *open* declaration of our heart to the Lord is, I find, fundamentally important for placing me in the right relationship to Him.

Second, it is important to confess Christ openly to others. Our baptism services provide opportunity for that to happen at conversion, but that only ritualises what we should be doing continually. All of us who work in bringing others to Christ know how helpful it is for those who have been newly won for His Kingdom to go and tell someone about their new faith. That open confession is a crucially important part of a person's awareness of their commitment to Christ. It usually *confirms* their allegiance to Him, in relationship to their world around. *The world now knows where I stand, and I know where I stand in the world.*

If that is the beginning of Jesus's lordship in our lives, I am sure that our present world with all its demands to serve other lords provides more than sufficient opportunity for all Christians to confess their allegiance to Jesus the Lord and to Him alone.

'There is another king; Jesus' (Acts 17:7).

This means that when there is a conflict of moral choices, Christians choose the Lord's, even if that is unpopular in the world's eyes, and even if it is something we might find difficult. It is *only* when we have placed ourselves in right relationship to the Lord by openly confessing Him that we shall have a clearer picture of who He is and what He can do in our lives.

When I confessed my love for my girlfriend, both she and I knew where we stood, and from then onwards our relationship developed into marriage. So, too, when I confess Jesus is Lord, both He and I know where we stand and our life together starts to grow.

When I confessed my love for my girlfriend, the world then soon learned there was some special relationship between us. Similarly, true confession of Jesus as our Lord leads inevitably to the world around knowing that we belong only to Him. Our minds are set on Him and no one else, and we are proud to be able to declare it.

But confession is not just about the true status of Jesus Christ. He indeed is Lord, but confessing that properly includes a heartfelt understanding of the relationship between the Lord and the one who confesses.

Isaiah saw the Lord and knew his own condition, and we, when we confess Jesus is Lord do so knowing that means *we are His subjects* – subjects who know their Lord has rightful authority over their lives. We have not really seen who Jesus is until we *know* He has total authority over us.

Immediately Elizabeth was crowned Queen of England, the lords of the realm knelt in front of her and swore their allegiance to her as their sovereign. If we believe that 'at the name of Jesus every knee should bow, in heaven and on earth and under the earth, and every tongue confess that Jesus Christ is Lord, to the glory of God the Father' (Phil. 2:10–11), then we, too, need to acknowledge He is sovereign over our lives.

The centurion in Matthew 8:5–13 truly understood who Jesus was, not only in recognising His Lordship but also His authority. 'Lord, I am not worthy to have you come under my roof; but only say the word, and my servant will be healed. For I am a man under authority, with soldiers under me'. (vv. 8–9).

Confession establishes and creates the right dimensions of the relationship between the Lord Jesus and ourselves. Perhaps true focusing on the Lord so that we have a clear picture of Him means no less than that He has total authority and control in our lives. A blurred picture would mean that He only had partial control of us, but the more of our lives we submit to Him, moving even closer to making Him the real lord in our lives, the more marked will be His transforming power in our minds and lives. Much of this book consists of working that out in detail, but before moving to that, we still have to apply the other two lessons Isaiah has taught us.

The Other Lessons: Confessing and Dealing with Sin

Isaiah also showed us that we must be cleansed from our sins. That process, too, begins with confession. Confession is used in the New Testament not to own up to our sins, but to *own our sins*, so that we might be released from them.

Let me explain a truth which every Christian knows: the truth that the Lord will not bless anyone who deliberately lives a life displeasing to Him. If we consider then that our lives know too little of the life of the Holy Spirit; if we know no joy, no love, no peace; if we have never brought anyone to Christ, never seen the wonder of a healing sign; in other words if we have never personally tasted something of our future hope, then first of all we should ask the Holy Spirit to show us if there is any sin in our lives. The shutters of sin may have closed our eyes to seeing the Lord clearly. There are other reasons why we might not experience the Lord's rule in our lives, but the most fundamental obstacle to the Spirit working is usually our own sin and that must be investigated at the outset.

Confession is *the* New Testament way to deal with our sins. Thus, 1 John 1:9: 'If we confess our sins, he is faithful and just, and will forgive our sins and cleanse us from all unrighteousness.' We have already seen that confession means declaring what our heart feels and knows about itself, and I cannot over-emphasise that sense of owning our sins as the necessary preliminary to becoming free of them.

As a boy I was brought up in a Catholic-type church, and as a ten-year-old, they used to teach us about what they called 'confession', and part of that training was the 'self-examination' which consisted of a list of about 200 possible offences against God, other people and myself. When I read them through, I could skip so easily through the list because as I thought then, none of those sins applied to me. Now, if I ever bother to pick up that list, I cannot read through a few before I am convicted of my sin. I have changed, by God's grace, to know my true state, I hope.

Many of us can slip into that boyhood mentality of not really taking sin that seriously. Perhaps we are aware of the things we say or think, but consider that in some sort of way, they are not really us. Yet we delude ourselves by thinking it wasn't really us when we were rude to our colleagues; we must have eaten something that upset us; a bad night's sleep perhaps; and 'anyway, didn't they deserve it?' I find there can be quite a spiritual battle going on inside me to accept that I am not as good as I like to think I am.

It is not until we *own* our sin that we can become free of it, and receive the first of all Christ's blessings, His forgiveness. Here is a trivial example from my own life.

For some years I was bogged down in my spiritual growth because I did not pray or read my Bible regularly. It was not that I did not want to, but I did not get around to it as I should. I found it an effort. At the same time, there was no great evidence that the Lord was blessing His work through me.

I would, of course, confess these neglects, and although I am sure the Lord was gracious enough to forgive me, I never experienced a change in my life style over a long period of time. The 'resolution' wore off. That is until one day, God's light dawned, and I realised that all these failures of God's business were simply due to my laziness. I was convicted of the sin of sloth. I wriggled a lot. 'Who, me? Slothful? Never! Look at all the work I put into that . . .'

The Holy Spirit was showing me my true state, but it was only when I accepted that as indeed being my true condition and confessed it that I was freed from both sloth and its effects.

But I had to own it. 'Pratt, you are slothful.' I had to accept that laziness was not on the periphery of my life, it was *in* my life.

Yet, even this owning is only the first part of the process, as necessary as it is. The next part of confession is open declaration. So, James 5:16, 'Therefore *confess your sins to one another'* (my italics). And Matthew 3:6, 'and they were baptized by him [John] in the river Jordan, *confessing their sins'* (my italics). Why then is it important to confess our sins out loud and even out loud to others?

In a comic-strip speech-bubble, a particular character says something and the words are encircled by a sort of string and attached to the speaker's mouth, like a bubble. But like a bubble, his speech is there, away from him. He has discharged what he was thinking, and his words, now bound by open declaration, are ready to float away. That's how speaking out our sins works. Confession becomes a means of distancing ourselves from our sins. Declaring what we are, means that we can look at them and point our finger at them, 'There they are – the destroyers of my soul!'

Yet like the speech-bubble they are still attached to our mouths, and we can swallow them all back again, unless someone pricks the bubble or takes it away. And that someone is Jesus Christ, who died to take away all our sins, 'who takes away the sin of the world' (John 1:29). But we have to confess first. Every Christian confession is to the Lord Jesus, because it is only He who is able to take our sins away, yet there are certain times when it is right to 'confess our sins to one another' as James directs.

I would recommend acting on this direction in these following conditions.

First of all, if after confessing your sins to the Lord privately, your conscience was still troubled over some grievous sin (indeed, I think I should follow James's advice if I had committed any grievous sin). Second, when we need *to hear* someone pray the Lord's forgiveness to us. We might need to hear that for the very human reason that our faith is low and we need assurance, or even that what we have done or thought was so vile that we need that spoken certainty of the Lord's forgiveness. (The irony is that people will confess easily relatively less serious sins like neglecting their Bible-study, but feel too ashamed about confessing their sin and guilt on problems like adultery and abortion, which in my experience *needs* the assurance of forgiveness!)

The Lord Jesus has given authority to His Church, telling the first disciples, 'If you forgive the sins of any, they are forgiven' (John 20:23). And certainly I for one need to hear that myself sometime in that personal way. Remember, the Lord's words are not empty. They always achieve what He sends them out to do. Consequently, when I hear someone say to me on the Lord's behalf, 'Your sins are forgiven', I receive them as Christ's power to release those sins from me instantly.

Most of the time, I am content to receive that word from Scripture itself, but there are those times when I need to hear those authoritative words of the Lord spoken out loud by someone else *who knows what I am*.

Open confession places us in right relationship with the Lord Jesus; He is the Saviour, I am a sinner. He died to save me from my sins and only He can rescue me, only He can take my sins away. That has to be done before anything else will happen. The old paint has to be scraped off before the new is applied.

The Christians in the Bible were ordinary people, they were special only in the sense that they show us what it can mean to live under the lordship of Christ more than perhaps some of us do.

There were the miracles, but they came out of their knowledge of who Jesus is. 'But Peter said, "I have no silver and gold, but I give you what I have; in the *name of Jesus Christ* of Nazareth, walk"' (Acts 3:6; my italics).

There was the community life. The peace and fellowship, the joy of our promised future came to earth in the first Christian colony in Jerusalem.

. . . and had all things in common; and they sold their possessions and goods and distributed them to all, as any had need. And day by day, attending the temple together and breaking bread in their homes, they partook of food with glad and generous hearts, praising God and having favour with all the people (Acts 2: 44–7).

Of course, the New Testament churches were not without their problems, but *they were people under the lordship of Jesus*, as is evidenced by their new way of thinking and living. They were being transformed! And that's our inheritance.

The next chapter looks at what the Lord does first to change us from our ways of living to His.

4

LEAVING THE OLD WAYS

I had noticed Dave a couple of times before when I made my occasional visits to the school. At that time I did not know him except by reputation. One thing I knew, however, was that his teachers were scared of him, and it was not surprising. He had a reputation of being very violent. He was a well-built mid-teenager. I used to see him prowling around the back of a class of pupils his teacher would be trying to control. He paced up and down the back of the classroom like a caged wild animal. I remember that even though it was a warm summer day he was walking up and down dressed in a dark overcoat with its collar turned up. It was a strange and disturbing sight, but I suppose it was safer for the teacher to let it happen. After all, this boy was known for his vicious temper and abusive tongue.

He was already on the fringes of criminality, already rubbing shoulders with the law, but on the wrong side. I had by that time an experienced ministry with such youngsters who seemed to be possessed by petty criminality. They seemed to express a youth culture which found its value in being as antisocial as possible, and although this was not usually manifested in physical violence, when alcohol was around it wasn't too far away. I had met scores of Daves. In our home we had given hospitality to many, and had discovered that the majority of them had very distressing family backgrounds. Trouble at home, trouble at school, trouble with the police. As far as most of the community around was concerned, that described them, they were 'trouble' with a capital 'T'.

At different times I had officiated at the funeral services of three or four of them; one had drowned in the local river in rumoured suspicious circumstances; one with some friends had stolen a car and was killed when they took a corner too fast; another under the influence of drugs literally danced under the wheels of an approaching car. The tragedies were endless. Without doubt, Dave was already on the road to self- and soul-destruction.

They needed saving, and my church believed the Lord had called us to bring His love to those teenagers and to show them that He was Saviour.

Our tactic was quite simple. Since such young men like Dave would never dream of going to church, then the church would have to go to them.

We met Dave when we were holding a week-end's tent mission on the housing estate where he and many more 'Daves' lived. On the Saturday evening we put on a 'coffee bar' – the traditional menu of coffee, chat, Gospel music and an invitation to accept Jesus Christ as Lord and Saviour.

I found myself in earnest dialogue with Dave and half a dozen or so of his friends. It was extremely difficult. They spent most of the time jeering at everything we said. Then, by some miracle, I knew the Holy Spirit was there. There was a pregnant silence. Dave broke it. He spoke up mockingly.

'All right, Mike,' he said, 'I'll give it a try.' They all laughed – it was a joke. He stood up and swaggered his shoulders, after all, this was the tough guy of the group.

'Dave,' I replied, 'dealing with God is a serious business. You must mean what you have to pray.'

'Oh that's okay,' was his reply, 'I'm serious enough.'

Instead of asking him to pray with me to give his life over to the Lord in front of his friends, I called over a young Christian who was helping that night.

'Phil,' I called, 'would you please take Dave over into that corner, away from his friends. He wants to submit his life to Jesus as his Lord.' There was a titter. Dave sauntered over into the far corner, just occasionally looking over his shoulder with a mocking smile at his friends. There, in the corner, he sat with Phil for some time.

I carried on talking to his friends. They were beginning to feel uncomfortable. They kept looking over their shoulders to see what was happening to Dave. Then he stood up, turned around and started his characteristic saunter back to us. A big grin came over his face and he said:

'Relax, folks. Nothing has happened to me. I haven't felt a thing.' They all laughed. It eased the tension.

'Dave,' I said, 'I wonder what you expected to happen. Anyway, we shall see, come and sit down.' The only vacant chair was at my side, so he sat by me and was therefore out of my eye-contact. I slogged on with the other boys. First of all, I was aware of the slog, then I became aware of that other boy at my side. Dave had grown quieter and quieter.

Suddenly he interrupted. He was not a very fluent speaker, but he had something very important on his mind.

'Mike,' he said, 'I've got this feeling inside me. I feel I've got to do something. Can you help me, please?'

'What's the problem, Dave?'

He replied, 'Last night, me and some of my gang broke into a house and stole lots of things. I have this feeling that I want to take what I stole back to the owners. But I don't know how to do it without getting my friends into trouble with the police. Can you help me do it please?'

The mouths of the others were open in sheer amazement!

'Of course, Dave,' I answered, 'I can arrange that. Why don't you go off and get what you stole and I will make sure it gets back.'

Off he went, and I turned to the others. They were stunned.

'Tell me,' I asked, 'has Dave ever given back anything he has stolen?'

'No,' they replied with one voice. 'Dave is so mean. He *never ever* gives anything back!'

'Well, then,' I pressed them. 'Who do you think changed him?' There was silence, but they all knew the answer. They had just witnessed a miracle, David had been changed by the Holy Spirit. There had been no feelings, no sense of joy, no feeling of love at that stage, those things were to come for Dave, but what had happened is that the Spirit of God had come into Dave and done the most important work of all. The Holy Spirit had, as it were, picked him up by the scruff of his neck, shown him how wrong his way of life was, put conviction into his heart, and then put him down on the straight and narrow way of the Lord Jesus. A spiritual revolution had happened. It is what the Scriptures call 'repentance'.

This chapter will tease out two components in repentance, the next chapter will look at another. Repentance is without doubt the first thing Christ's transforming presence works in us, moving us from where we are in our ways to relating to life in His.

But before looking at the two components of repentance, I must first dispel what repentance is not. I must do that because I have found the following misunderstandings undermine what the Lord wants to do in us.

First of all, *repentance is not just being sorry for one's moral failings and sins*. Of course, repentance could well include being sorry and to some extent it should, but there is something far deeper involved. The danger of equating repentance with sorrow for moral failure is that we all too easily recognise that people like Dave obviously need Christ to work in them. Today's society disapproves of their way of life. Their behaviour is antisocial, and everyone wags their finger at them.

But what about the respectable?

Sin has I as its middle letter.

What about the law-abiding?

What about people like you and me: What makes us think that our ways of life and our understanding are so God-centred? I wonder how many of us pride ourselves on our success and happiness through our self-determination, self-reliance and self-motivation? Are not those successful 'selfs' humanly applauded as they are, so often, *our* soul's stumbling-block? Remember, Adam and Eve were not thrown out of the Garden because they were petty criminals, but because they ate the fruit 'wanting to be like God'. They asserted themselves. Sin has 'I' as its middle letter!

It does not matter if the road we are travelling on is in the opposite direction to God's or a few degrees away, in the end, both miss Him.

We must never think that repentance is only needed by those who have done terrible things – if you like, the Daves of this world. Perhaps it's people with self-assertive, self-determined life styles who bring more long-term harm to other people and the world's environment than any Dave.

Second, repentance is not 'putting people under law'. That is jargon, but it means making people conform to accepted Christian ways of living. People form 'group identity' through their shared beliefs, values and codes of behaviour. Have you ever noticed how someone behaves when they come to church for the first time? They really want to know what to do so they do not feel left out. They keep an eye on those nearby so they know when to sit and stand at the appropriate times, and if something happens in the service when everybody else except them knows what to do, they will probably feel embarrassed and even alienated. After all, we like to do what everybody else does and feel part of it.

It's true to say that the more we want to belong to something, the more likely it is that we shall want to conform with the way things are done.

So if new Christians come to our churches, they may

well be asking a normal human question: 'What do you have to do and say to belong to this group of people called Christians?'

But those who answer, 'This is what Christians do: They go to church. They read their Bibles. They tithe their income. They pray. They help other people. They do not smoke. They do not drink. They are chaste,' are giving a *merely* human answer. Since our enquirer wants to belong, he or she will do their best to conform. They might even be successful in conforming.

But this is not repentance. It is will power. It is akin to New Year resolutions, when we declare we shall *try* better.

Now, if someone is well-endowed with will power, I am sure they will in time put on all the outward trappings of being a good and sincere Christian. But if someone is not so well-endowed with will power, and especially if they are in the grip of a strong passion for something or someone, they will simply be unable to hold to what they believe Christians should be doing, and they will feel condemned by their inevitable failure. Please note, *conformity is not the same as repentance.*

The Lord Jesus had some very strong things to say to the Pharisees who confused conformity to religious rules with repentance.

> Woe to you, teachers of the law and Pharisees, you hypocrites! You are like whitewashed tombs, which look beautiful on the outside but on the inside are full of dead men's bones and everything unclean. In the same way, on the outside you appear to people as righteous but on the inside you are full of hypocrisy and wickedness (Matt. 23:27–8 NIV).

Of course all of those codes of behaviour are important, but they have to be wrought in us by the Holy Spirit and not by the pressure of the community.

Repentance means Decision

Decision is the first component in repentance that I want to examine. When Dave experienced the Lord turning his life upside-down, he was left with a decision – to follow Christ and return the things he had stolen. He would not have repented unless he had made that decision.

In my ministry I have brought many people to the point of submitting their lives to Jesus, but they have declined to decide for Him. I have been quite convinced they have caught a real glimpse of who Jesus is, and have appreciated the misery or sheer dullness of their own lives. I remember one man who saw all that clearly. He asked me: 'What do I have to do now?'

I answered: 'Submit yourself to the Lord Jesus and ask Him to be the Lord and Saviour of your life.'

He paused for a couple of minutes, and replied, 'I am sorry, I cannot do that.' He would not decide for the Lord.

The Lord leaves that decision entirely in our hands, but one thing is certain, it is only as we decide for Him that we can enter His transforming presence.

As I look out of my window, the sky is overcast. It is a typically grey English day. But over there, some miles away, there is a dash of blue sky and the sun is gloriously shining through. My children, being fed up with the rain, want to go over there to the sunshine. 'Why can't we go over there, Dad, where the sky is blue? There is sunshine over there!' They know they can only get over there if they can make me decide to drive them over there.

They see the truth of the matter. Here it is miserable. There it is glorious. But to get there needs a decision.

Apply that to understanding something of the meaning of repentance. When we first met the Lord Jesus personally He broke through into our life and gave us a taste of what life is like with Him. But that experience came initially as a dash of blue sky in the overcast greyness of our lives. We were so attracted by Him that we decided to go to Him. We 'turned to Christ'. We made a personal decision for Him.

That initial decision for Christ is an action we must continue to make. It is all very well knowing that it is wonderful when the Lord is present in our lives, but how many of us are in fact living under the grey clouds of everyday existence and can only point 'over there' to the time when we were converted, or filled with the Holy Spirit? It is worth asking ourselves about the *quality* of our lives as Christians. Do we genuinely know His love in our hearts? Do we know His peace and joy? Are we where He is, or are we in our old ways of life pointing to the Lord Jesus somewhere over there?

Repentance means Leaving the Old Ways

Deciding to be with Jesus means leaving our old ways. Sometimes people have to do just that. Dave had to leave a way of life of petty criminality.

The rich young man who asked what he must do to inherit eternal life was told, 'Sell what you have, and give to the poor, and you will have treasure in heaven; and come, follow me' (Mark 10:21).

Do you remember how Peter said to Jesus, 'Lord we have *left* everything to follow you'? Again and again in the stories of the New Testament we hear how Jesus's followers left everything to follow him. It started with the shepherds on the Bethlehem hills leaving their flocks to seek out the child in swaddling clothes. It continued with the fishermen leaving their nets and following Jesus who promised to make them 'fishers of men'. It finds another focus in St Paul, who wrote:

> But whatever gain I had, I counted as loss for the sake of Christ. Indeed I count everything as loss because of the surpassing worth of knowing Christ Jesus my Lord. For his sake I have suffered the loss of all things,

and count them as refuse, in order that I may gain Christ . . .' (Phil. 3:7–8).

They are all people who left ways of life and found the joy of being with the Lord Jesus. Of course, the Lord does not ask all of us to leave our jobs, homes and families. *Leaving* is not particularly the action of walking out, rather it *is the resolve that our old life, no matter what it is, will no longer control or shape the way we think and behave.*

We should, of course, all acknowledge that God's Holy Spirit does not shine on a life of criminality or immorality. '. . . neither the immoral, nor idolators, nor adulterers, nor sexual perverts, nor thieves, nor the greedy, nor drunkards, nor revilers, nor robbers, will inherit the kingdom of God' (1 Cor. 6:9–10). The Gospel call is 'repent' and leave those sorts of life.

But there is another truth. Many of us have to abandon and leave *attitudes* and the underlying assumptions which support our chosen styles of living. I have had to leave a way of life of middle-class *self*-motivation, *self*-confidence and *self*-ability. There was nothing morally wrong with what I was doing with my life except that I was doing it. If the Holy Spirit does not bless an obviously immoral way of life, neither does He bless a life of pride, self-assertion, power-seeking, lukewarm spirituality, materialism, middle-class contentedness, *nor any other life style which is based on the standards of this world*. If our life is based on anything away from God, we shall never know the richness of His presence in our life. God does not exist to approve or applaud *our* chosen life style, and like the so-called immoral, we too have to realise that compared with what the Lord wants us to have, our life style is barren.

This is true of our personal lifestyles and the way we respond to life. It is also true of the values and assumptions we have soaked in from our host culture. We have already seen that whether we like it or not, we are children of secularism. We have learnt to understand and respond to life as if there was no God. Secularism holds us, and to some great extent or other, has fashioned our minds.

'Leaving' challenges us to renounce *all* these godless ways of thinking about our world and move to Christ's.

The Book of Common Prayer puts it like this in the baptism service.

> Dost thou renounce the devil and all his works, the vain pomp and glory of the world, with all its covetous desires of the same, and the carnal desires of the flesh, so that thou wilt not follow, nor be led by them.
> Answer: I renounce them all.

If we desire to have a new mind which sees and beholds the wonders of God, both in the future and in this world, we, too, must be prepared to *leave all* and go where the Lord asks us to go. When we have focused clearly on the Lord, He will make demands.

If you have to renounce a good middle-class understanding of life, you will have to do it.

If you have to renounce your intellectual abilities, you will have to do it.

If you have to renounce your standard of living, you will have to do it.

You have no choice if that is what your vision of God demands of you, and the Lord will ask you to leave anything which blocks His rule in your life. Please do not read anything here as merely another exhortation to try better. It is only the Holy Spirit Himself who shows us the total barrenness of *any* life style which is not truly focused on the Lord. He, the Holy Spirit, convicts and convinces us of our sin, and although you might have been challenged by what you have read, it will only be when the Holy Spirit has shown *you* the truth of it that you will desire to renounce all and turn away from it to the life of Christ.

But I can assure you, if you genuinely confess that

Jesus is your Lord, it will not be too long before He demands you *leave* where you are and move into His light.

I have to say that nothing, no matter how much it is valued by the world or even ourselves, is exempt. The Holy Spirit trains us to renounce them all and to turn to Christ (Titus 2).

Dave, by the way, is now a remarkable Christian young man. It is some years since his conversion, but he is now in Christ's light. He is a source of strength and inspiration for other Christians. He has been used in the healing ministry. He has a prophetic gift. He can form good, loyal relationships. By God's grace, he renounced his old way of life and let the Holy Spirit take him to where Christ's glory shines.

The next chapter describes what God does to give us a new mind.

5

THE MIND-CHANGING EVENT

Did you ever see the cartoon of two caterpillars talking to each other as they watched a butterfly fluttering overhead? One caterpillar said to the other: 'You won't get me up there in one of those contraptions.'

Someone had not taught it about metamorphosis – the process through which caterpillars change their total form from being creepy-crawlies into one of the most delightful creatures in God's world. A butterfly is not a caterpillar with a couple of wings fixed to its back, rather it has come into being because of a deep transformation of its whole nature. In fact, that is what the word 'metamorphosis' means, because it comes from two Greek works *'meta'* which means 'change' and *'morphosis'* meaning 'shaping or moulding'.

You can see this when you watch a potter working at his wheel. He throws a lump of shapeless clay on to the wheel and fashions it into a vase, but then, changing his mind, uses his skills to shape a curved plate. The plate is as different from the vase as the butterfly is from the caterpillar. They are both examples of that deep change we call metamorphosis. This chapter is about another sort of deep and radical change, another *'meta'*. It is about a change of mind. Now, we talk freely about changing our minds. Someone asks us if we should like a cup of tea, and we answer that we don't, but then we shout out: 'Put the kettle on, Mary. I've changed my mind about that cup of tea.'

What we mean is that we have simply changed our

decision, but what I hope you have learned in this book is that mind means far more than the decisions we make. Our minds determine how we see and understand our world and direct us as to how we are to respond to what we see and hear. Formed by the various forces discussed in the first chapter, they are the spectacles through which we see and respond to everything. This chapter is about having a different way in perceiving, understanding and relating to the world around.

I know someone who is a socialist. His whole outlook is formed and fashioned by socialist doctrines. When he reads the newspapers or watches television, he interprets and responds to everything according to his left-wing opinions. Imagine what it is like when he meets someone who holds opposite views as strongly. The sparks really fly! But now consider the impossible; one morning, our socialist friend wakes up and renounces all his previous ideas and ways of thinking and embraces the right-wing outlook of his former opponent. If such a thing could happen, that, too, would be an example of what it means to 'change our mind'. Our ex-socialist would now look at the world through different-coloured spectacles.

Some years ago we had a very large garden, in fact, it was rather too big to manage properly. I did my best, but I never really found the time to tackle a patch of weeds and nettles which were out of sight of the house. I used to feel somewhat guilty and ashamed of that weed patch until I had a change of mind, indeed until I was 'converted' to see things differently. All the credit goes to my brother-in-law. Every so often, he with his family and friends would descend upon our country vicarage as they were on their way to their holiday. They lived in the smarter rural band around London, and were well up in the latest fashion. They came down to our home, poking around its early nineteenth-century nooks and crannies and then they descended into the garden for a grand inspection.

'Oh no,' I thought, 'I wonder what they will say about my weeds and nettles.' I was also aware of a rising sense of shame and failure as a gardener. But they returned brimming over with enthusiasm.

'Mike,' they beamed, 'how marvellous! How long have you had that patch of natural garden?'

'Natural garden? Whatever do they mean?' I wondered. Then I realised they were talking about my 'weed patch'!

My weeds and nettles were no longer ample evidence of my failure as a gardener, but rather examples of my sensitivity to the ecological needs of insects and butterflies. What a marvellously different way of seeing things. I was instantly converted.

Greek has a '*meta*' word for this change of mind as it has a '*meta*' word for change of shape. The word is '*metanoia*'. '*Meta*' means 'change' and '*noia*' comes from the word for mind '*noos*'. (*Noos* or *nowse* will be familiar to readers from the north of England, for they might have heard people say 'Do you have any nowse, lad?' – meaning do they have any commonsense.)

Of course it is true to say that though we use metamorphosis to describe part of the life-cycle of insects, we do not use *metanoia* to describe a radical change of mind. What we do, in fact, is to translate it by the word 'repentance'. We have seen that repentance includes leaving our old ways of life, confessing our sins, but it is imperative to grasp that the fundamental meaning of repentance is that transformation of our minds. A repentant person has a new and different way of perceiving and relating to him or herself and to the world around. This would show itself in the fruits of repentance, that is, a way of life which is centred on Christ, but more of that later.

Here is a clear example of a complete mind-change which happened to someone who was staying with us. We used to belong to a scheme of hosting overseas visitors to our country. They were always young adults and they would live with us for a month or so and share our home-life. On one of these visits, a young Swiss man, called Hans-Peter, stayed with us. He was a nice, polite fellow, but he believed there was no God. He had been raised in a humanist home. His family was wealthy. His father ran a business and his mother was a child psychologist. He was healthy and well-balanced, and had been brought up to believe that there was no God. That was his stance, his view, his mind about life. He did not go around proclaiming his atheism, he simply saw life atheistically. As far as he was concerned, there was no God to see, so he did not even bother to look.

In those days we had an extensive ministry to young people who came and went to our home very regularly, even staying with us for days at a time. Most of these young people were committed Christians, so Hans-Peter was continually surrounded by others who saw things very differently. He was never intimidated by any of this, in fact he was humanly curious to find more about those around him. He came to church, attended the discussion groups and went with them on their various fun trips. One evening he joined us all for a praise-and-prayer meeting in our house. There were, I suppose, twenty or so late teenagers flopped around in a circle, gently praying and praising God. Quite suddenly, Hans-Peter burst into tears and ran out of the room. Someone who spoke German dashed out after him, and after what seemed like hours, Hans-Peter returned. It was obvious that he wanted to say something.

'May I please explain? All of my life, I have been brought up to think that you Christians were wrong in what you believe, and that I was right. Tonight, I realised it is you who are right, and that it is I who was wrong. My whole way of thinking has been turned completely upside-down. That reversal was so sudden and unexpected that it was extremely disturbing for me emotionally, and that was why I cried.'

Hans-Peter had just undergone that mind-changing

operation we call repentance. He had been given a new mind.

St Paul must have been somewhat of an expert on this subject, because on the road to Damascus, he, too, underwent a tremendous mind transformation. Paul was committed to eliminating the New Testament church. Having already supervised the execution of the first Christian martyr, Stephen, he had authority to arrest members of the Christian sect who lived in Damascus. But there on the road to Damascus, the risen Jesus appeared to him, and he was converted into being one of the Christian faith's greatest missionaries. The story is told in Acts 9.

When we look at this story in detail we see all the familiar factors which operate in any mind-change transformation. First of all, Paul already had a definite outlook on the world. His mind had been fashioned and formed through the teachings and influence of the Pharisees. He wrote about himself, 'circumcised on the eighth day, of the people of Israel, of the tribe of Benjamin, a Hebrew born of Hebrews; as to the law a Pharisee, as to zeal a persecutor of the church' (Phil. 3:5–6).

Paul, the orthodox Jew, believed that it was his people and only they who were God's chosen race. He would have held such a belief with deep conviction, for after all it was based on God's promises going back to Abraham, the father of the Jews. It would have been inconceivable for someone like Paul even to consider that uncircumcised non-Jews (the Gentiles) could stand before God as equals with the Jews. There can be no doubt that Paul was a sincere, devout and orthodox Jew, not only in accepting the beliefs of Judaism, but because he lived what they taught. Consequently, according to his own testimony he was zealous in persecuting the church. Since such zeal usually arises from a deep conviction that what we are doing is absolutely right, Paul must have been sure that what the first Christians claimed about the crucified and resurrected Messiah was not only wrong, but was extremely dangerous and indeed blasphemous. So no wonder we read in the Acts of the Apostles:

> But Saul [Paul] still breathing threats and murder against the disciples of the Lord, went to the high priest, and asked him for letters to the synagogues at Damascus, so that if he found any belonging to the Way, men or women, he might bring them bound to Jerusalem (9:1–2).

Paul's mind was set.

Then he met the Lord. Just notice how dramatic that change of mind was.

He who was previously jealous of the privilege of the Jewish people became the great Apostle to the Gentile world. Paul wrote, 'those, I say, who were of repute added nothing to me; but on the contrary, when they saw that I had been entrusted with the gospel to the uncircumcised . . .' (Gal. 2:6–7).

We should not underestimate Paul's change of direction in ministry as merely stemming from his obedience to his vision of Christ on the Damascus road. Motivation, certainly Paul's style of motivation, derives from our personal insight into what we believe to be true, and the fact is that Paul's whole way of looking at things was turned upside-down. His energy and drive stemmed from that repentance. We only have to read his letters to the Christians in Rome and Galatia to realise that he perceived his former Jewish traditions in a very different light. In fact the thrust of his letters is to oppose with all his might any tendency to bring the New Testament Christians under the Jewish legal systems. He knows with all his heart that it was those traditions which had blinded him from recognising God's love and grace working in Jesus's disciples like Stephen, and if that was not enough, he knows, too, that it was people who sincerely held those beliefs who, not recognising God's presence in Jesus, had rejected Him and handed Him over for crucifixion.

There can be no doubt that Saul on the Damascus road and Paul in Damascus were two different people, different in that a mind-changing event had happened. The Lord Jesus had turned Paul inside out. Paul was so different that his zeal, directed into spreading the good news of the Christian faith, got him into trouble immediately. It was not long before he had disturbed his opponents enough for them to plot to kill him. When he arrived back in Jerusalem, the disciples there could not believe that he really had changed that much. Paul had truly undergone a transformation of his mind. Whether the mind-changing event was as dramatic as Paul's or as gentle as Hans-Peter's, the result was the same. They both ended up thinking and behaving in ways which they did not do before because they saw things differently. That is repentance.

How Repentance Works

It is true to say that for some people such mind-changing events are 'V-shaped' experiences. Like Paul, there was a definite moment in time, a definite encounter, and life's direction *suddenly* changed course. But the same change also happens through 'U-shaped experiences', where there has been a gradual change in direction.

However, sudden or gradual change as it may be, any change in direction can only happen if something and some power makes it happen. We need something to make it happen. In fact, that is one of the most fundamental laws of science. 'A body keeps going in the same direction until a force acts upon it to change its direction.' This is very true as far as changing our minds is concerned. We shall keep thinking the way we do until another power acts upon our minds, causing them to change direction.

It seems to me that when I think about people like Hans-Peter, there have been two sources of the same power at work. First of all, they have been exposed to the Holy Spirit working in and through those around them, the source of power has been *outside* themselves. Second, there has been an internal revolution when power has acted *inside* them.

The Power Outside

When someone is converted, it is likely that one or more major reasons for their change has been one of the following *external factors*:

1. They *heard* a clear presentation of the Christian faith.
2. They *saw* that people who say they are Christians really do love one another.
3. They *saw* someone healed instantly of some disease.
4. They *saw* a loved one converted and have been impressed by that change.
5. They *read* something in the Bible or a faith-inspiring book.
6. They *heard* a clear witness to faith from a friend.
7. They *looked* at the stars one night and were overwhelmed with awe.
8. They *saw* how someone was coping with pain and suffering.
9. They *saw* the peace and harmony in a Christian's home.
10. Like Paul, they had a vision.

The list is endless, but the point is that something was going on *out there* which had power to declare God was present. It is as if their ears, having heard the evangelist telling them of God's love, addressed their minds: 'What do you think about this? Have you heard of that sort of thing before?'

I am sure our five senses receive all outside stimuli, but

our minds have learned to select what information it thinks is relevant.

Nevertheless, I believe minds are made to relate to the *whole* realm of information they receive, so the more God-centred events they are subjected to, the more likely it will be that they will try and make sense of them. Our minds cope quite well with experiencing the odd miracle or two by usually deeming them as 'co-incidences', but when there is a flood of such external factors, our minds can either raise their floodgates of doubt and disbelief to prevent those powerful things entering, or they can let the information in and take the consequences of having to think through their way of understanding the world. Such events are power sources which can turn our minds; they can bring repentance.

That is why full-blooded evangelism will proclaim the good news both in words and actions, for by so doing it will provide stimuli for all the senses. Eyes, ears, touch, smell, taste will declare to the unconverted mind, 'What do you think about this?' So, not surprisingly, when the Lord Jesus commissioned the twelve disciples, he told them to minister to both sight and hearing: 'And preach as you go, saying, "The kingdom of heaven is at hand. Heal the sick, raise the dead, cleanse lepers, cast out demons"' (Matt. 10:7–8).

The Power Within

It would be quite wrong to think that powerful events happening outside us were all that was necessary for people to have changed minds. The Old Testament knows too well that mighty miracles performed for the good of the people may make no impression at all. The Israelites experienced many marvels when they were rescued from Egypt. They were rescued from death at the Passover, they walked dry-shod through the Red Sea, they were fed miraculously in the desert on manna and quails, but they still remained hard-hearted and rebellious. We should think of the ways God addresses our minds through our senses as a softening-up process. As our minds are bombarded with such unusual events, they soon realise that they have no means to understand what is happening. It is this confusion which should then lead us to *ask God to give us a mind* which can make sense of all these things. No one can perform a heart-transplant operation on themselves, and neither can anyone perform this radical change of mind, this *metanoia*, this repentance, on themselves.

King David realised this. In Psalm 51 he prayed: 'Behold, thou desirest truth in the inward being; therefore *teach me wisdom* in my secret heart' (v. 6; my italics) and then he went on to pray, 'Create in me a clean heart, O God, and put a new and right spirit within me' (v. 10).

David knows the impossibility of changing his heart himself, but he knows that the power for repentance rests in God alone. The source of change is not within us, nor under our control. Repentance, God's power to work that *mind-change within us*, is in His hands, and we receive it by *gift*.

For St Luke, particularly, repentance is a gift of God. In Acts 5:31, he recorded what St Peter said to the High Priest: 'God exalted him [Jesus] at his right hand as Leader and Saviour, *to give repentance* to Israel and forgiveness of sins' (my italics).

In Acts 11:18, he tells how Peter had baptised Gentiles into the Christian faith after the Holy Spirit had fallen upon them. When Peter's Jewish critics heard what had happened, 'They glorified God, saying, "Then to the Gentiles also God has *granted repentance* unto life"' (my italics). They, too, knew repentance is a gift of God.

Decision; leaving old ways; the mind-change, are the three dimensions of repentance, and all are required. We are responsible for the first two, only God can create the third, and we can only receive it as a gift from Him.

St Luke writes that repentance is linked with baptism,

because St Peter felt compelled to baptise with water after he had recognised that the Holy Spirit had come. Perhaps the baptism rite symbolically demonstrates how the Holy Spirit is given to us to work repentance. Let us then begin with the one who first linked repentance and baptism, John the Baptist.

> I baptize you with water for repentance, but he who is coming after me . . . will baptize you with the Holy Spirit and with fire (Matt. 3:11).

> John the Baptiser appeared in the wilderness, preaching a baptism of repentance for the forgiveness of sins (Mark 1:4).

Traditionally, John the Baptist straddles both the Old and New Testaments for he proclaimed his message as the last prophet of the Old, but pointed to and prepared the way for Jesus the bringer of the New. As a prophet who knew God's message was communicated through all the senses, John proclaimed his message by word and deed, and the action which was distinctive of his ministry was, of course, baptism.

But what exactly was John proclaiming to the people through baptism? Was he giving them forgiveness of their sins in his ritual wash, or was he preparing them for what God was going to do in the immediate future? The Gospels portray John as the preparer and pointer to Jesus, so his baptism should best be understood as a symbolic action pointing to the future baptism of Spirit and fire from above that the Messiah, the Christ, will bring. John's baptism was a prophetic action pointing to what God is going to do. John called it a 'baptism for repentance'. It is a phrase which may well point to some extent to what was happening in those who were coming to the River Jordan, but it is as likely that it *points to a future 'mind-change'* which will happen in us when the Holy Spirit falls into our lives. John demonstrated with water how the Holy Spirit would fall and create a new mind in the believer.

When St Paul arrived in Ephesus (Acts 19:1f.), he found some disciples who had not even heard about the Holy Spirit. They had only received John's baptism which looked to the mind-change granted by God through the work of His Holy Spirit. Consequently, they were baptised in the name of the Lord Jesus, and the Holy Spirit came upon them after Paul had prayed for them. John the Baptist therefore proclaimed that repentance will be worked in us by the Holy Spirit when He comes in power upon us. Only when that happens will anyone know and understand the ways of God and see Him in all things.

So how can we receive God's gift of repentance? We receive it when the Holy Spirit comes into us, creating that new mind since it is only He who 'will teach you all things, and bring to your remembrance all that I have said to you' (John 14:26).

But *where* do we have to go to receive this gift? John did not invent baptism, for it was apparently in use as a ritual wash for Gentile converts to the Jewish faith, but he did something different with it. He insisted that everyone, including the Jews, should be baptised.

St Matthew records, 'Then *went out to him* Jerusalem and all Judea and all the region about the Jordan, and they were baptized by him in the river Jordan, confessing their sins' (3:55–6; my italics).

Yet John testifies, 'I baptize you with water; but he who is mightier than I is coming, the thong of whose sandals I am not worthy to untie; he will baptize you with the Holy Spirit and with fire' (Luke 3:16).

John points people to the Lord Jesus. What he is doing with water is symbolic of what the Lord will do with the Holy Spirit. As they came out to him for water baptism, they must go to Jesus to be baptised in the Holy Spirit. That's why John was overjoyed to hear that Jesus was baptising more people than himself. 'Rabbi, he who was with you beyond the Jordan, to whom you bore witness, here he is, baptising, and *all are going to him*' (John 3:26; my italics).

The Lord Jesus is the baptiser of the Holy Spirit, so *we must all go to Him* to receive the gift of repentance.

St Peter declared to the crowd at Pentecost, 'Being *exalted at the right hand of God*, and having received from the Father the promise of the Holy Spirit, he has poured out this which you see and hear' (Acts 2:33; my italics).

The Spirit comes from the throne of God. It is the gift of the King.

If we then desire the gift, let us be mindful of the giver! We approach the Lord Jesus, confessing Him, aware of our own sinfulness and need for change.

Finally, John the Baptist teaches that we must *submit ourselves* to the baptiser. When the people came to him for baptism, whether they were immersed or drenched from above, they put themselves into his hands or were under his hand. They had symbolically placed themselves under his authority. No one can baptise themselves. Someone always has to do it for us. It is submission.

All that is true for Christian baptism. It is only as we submit ourselves to the Lord Jesus's authority, putting ourselves into His hands, that we can receive the Holy Spirit. We receive the mind-change, God's gift of repentance by going to and submitting ourselves to the Lord.

This deeper understanding of repentance is not simply about morality or being sorry and promising not to do anything wrong again. Of course, it may well include such things, but if that was all repentance was about, there would be no need for the righteous and the law-abiding to repent because they would have nothing to repent from. If, however, repentance is about a radically new way of perceiving life, seeing everything stemming from, depending on, and accountable to God, then every human being needs that working of the Holy Spirit to transform their mind. One of the greatest misunderstandings about who or what is a Christian is that which defines someone as a Christian because they do good for others. I am not sure what Jews or even atheists would make of that! Yet, John the Baptist's message of repentance is directed to both good and bad, for the test of anyone's need of repentance is never the goodness or badness of their lives, but their lack of centredness on God. Consequently, so-called 'good people' need to repent as much as sinners and evil-doers. Jesus himself underlined that necessity when he was asked about some apparently innocent deaths. He replied:

> Do you think that these Galileans were worse sinners than all the other Galileans, because they suffered thus? I tell you, No; but unless you repent you will all likewise perish (Luke 13:2–3).

Perhaps the greatest need at this present time is to call the people of God into this work of repentance. At the first Christian Pentecost, the great crowd gathered around Peter and the Apostles were devout Jews and God-fearers. They were religious people on pilgrimage in Jerusalem. The crowd gathered because they had heard the Lord being praised enthusiastically in their own languages. They heard Peter proclaim the good news. *God's power was at work outside all those who were there.* All those events demanded of their minds, 'Now what do you think about this?' The Holy Spirit was at work, softening them, so no wonder they were 'cut to the heart'. After all, they had been blind to recognising God at work in Jesus. They were confused, they had no frame of reference, no one had ever thought God would act through a crucified Christ, so they asked: 'Brethren, what shall we do?' Peter replied, '*Repent* and be baptized every one of you . . .' (Acts 2:37–8; my italics).

They had to leave their old ways of life, they had to turn away from any sin, but they also had to *receive* God's gift of repentance. John the Baptist's ministry pointed to the *future* when the Holy Spirit would work repentance in us, but ever since Pentecost when that same Spirit fell on to the first disciples, Christian baptism has of necessity included the actual falling of the Holy Spirit on to the believer. The Gospel call is always 'Repent and believe', and that is a message to let the Holy Spirit come into our lives and transform our minds radically.

6

THE MIND-CHANGING PROCESS

> . . . you must no longer live as the Gentiles do, in the
> futility of their minds; they are darkened in their
> understanding, alienated from the life of God, because
> of the ignorance that is in them due to their hardness of
> heart . . . You did not so learn Christ! – assuming that
> you have heard about him and were taught in him . . .
> Put off your old nature . . . *and be renewed in the spirit of
> your minds* (Eph. 4:17–23; my italics).

It is comforting to realise that St Paul wrote that exhortation to a New Testament church. Neither is it the only
place where we find similar commands. Paul wrote in his
letter to the Romans, 'be transformed by the renewal of
your mind' (12:2), and we read in the Colossians letter
'have put on the new nature, which is *being renewed* in
knowledge . . . (3:10; my italics). I am glad to announce
to myself as well as to you that *God's work of repentance*, by
which we are totally and completely transformed in
mind, does not happen instantly, once and for all time.
Rather, God works in us by a *process*.

The New Testament teaches that Christians have
everything, all the blessings of heaven, 'in Christ', but
confusingly there are also many instructions about how
to receive what we already have! St Paul, for example,
could write to the Corinthians, 'in every way you were
enriched in him' (1 Cor. 1:5), 'so that you are not lacking
in any spiritual gift' (v. 7) and at 2:16 'we have the mind of
Christ', but he could not possibly have meant that *they* of

all churches, with their well-founded reputation of immorality and disorder, could actually be seeing life with renewed lives and minds! In fact, the major part of his first letter to the Corinthians is about telling them, sometimes in strong words, to put their house in order.

There is another example of this 'having it, yet not having it', in Paul's letter to the Colossians. He states very clearly what they are already in Christ: 'For you *have died*, and your life is hid with Christ in God' (Col. 3:3; my italics), but then he writes almost straight away, '*Put to death* therefore what is earthly in you' (v. 5; my italics).

Let us try and make sense of these two apparently conflicting statements:

But we have the mind of Christ (1 Cor. 2:16).
. . . be renewed in the spirit of your minds (Eph. 4:23).

Paul seems to be exhorting Christians *to become what they already have in Christ*. Perhaps it might help to resolve this tension if we look at a very ordinary human event – marriage. On the wedding day, the bride and the groom make tremendously solemn promises to one another. You give everything you are as a person to your partner.

You say, 'I will', so you give over your will, the gateway of your mind.

You give 'your solemn oath', so you give over your heart, your emotional and mental life. You give everything which makes you as a person tick.

You give 'your body', symbolised by the ring, but including everything your body needs.

It is a total commitment to your partner. You make those promises to your loved one in God's presence. They make the same promise to you. Then the minister or priest pronounces these most solemn of all words: 'Those whom God has joined together, let no man put asunder.'

In God's sight, man and woman *have become one flesh*. As far as He is concerned, 'one flesh' is what we are from then on.

But those of us who have been married, will know that for the rest of married life, the couple will be working on their relationship to make it become what God has already said it is. We have to become what we already are!

When my wife and I were engaged, I remember thinking, in all sincerity, that I knew all there was to know about love and developing a marriage. (Perhaps you have to feel like that to dare take the risk!) I have no doubt that we, in common with all couples, gave our whole selves to one another in the wedding ceremony. Yet, the reality is that such giving over has to be worked out in the graft of everyday life. Yes, we gave over our thoughts and emotions, but we soon discovered many areas of our life which we had not actually given to our partners. We committed our will, but we soon found that we wanted stubbornly to hang on to our independence and have our own way at the expense of our relationship; and of course we discovered other things about ourselves. Still, we *are* one flesh; *married life is becoming what we are in God's sight.* Unfortunately, there are some couples who never seem able to tackle the realisms of married life, but many, perhaps a great majority, do. They work at their marriage. They deal with difficult areas, bringing them openly before one another. They resolve conflicts or learn to live with differences. Every marriage finds its own way to do all of that, but by so doing it creates a *process* of becoming that 'oneness' which God has declared it to be.

The truth which concerns us, however, is that through St Paul's writing, God has declared 'we have the mind of Christ'. *That declaration is as certain as any proclamation about marriage unity.* Yet the truth of what we are has to become a reality in our lives. Indeed, Christ's mind, the renewed mind, is something we all have, yet like a newly-married couple who have to become what they are, so, too, we have to work with the Lord Jesus to move towards what is already ours.

Of course you could ask why the Lord takes so long

over renewing our minds and why he does not instantly and permanently transform them in 'the twinkling of an eye', but my answer would again be derived from our own experiences of growing deeper into relationship. It is *we* who need time – time to work out our relationships – time to see through the implications of new insights and self-revelation – time to integrate different ways of relating to others.

It is rather like baking a cake. Once the mixed ingredients are in the oven, the last thing we do is to apply all the energy needed to bake it in a fraction of a second. That would only produce a burnt disaster. No, when we bake, we bake over an extended period at the correct rate to ensure all the necessary culinary changes in the cake happen at the right speed. Then, we have a nice cake to eat! It is true with us in our relationships. Too much, too soon, even though it may be right, can be disaster for us.

I remember one marriage that went through a very difficult patch. The wife had joined a training course for in-depth counselling. During one of the sessions with the psychotherapists, she came to the conclusion that the reason why she married was that she was really wanting another father. She came home that same evening and shared what she thought she had discovered about herself with her husband. It did not do an awful lot of good for them! It was too much, too soon. All of us need time to work out the implications of new insights, because some of those revelations could well strike down into the deepest part of our being. That woman, for example, had treated that 'insight' as mere knowledge, something like knowing that Paris is the capital city of France. Yet, it was an insight which, if true, would strike deep into her childhood relationship with her father. It would have changed her whole being very radically if she had let it work through. Consider her husband, too. How many of us would cope with an instant piece of information that our partner had not married 'me', but their picture of their father or mother in me. Of course, such things may be true in part for many people, but insights like these take time and have their own pace of working through us.

I suggest then that the Lord does not renew our minds in the 'twinkling of an eye', because we could not cope with such a dramatic change. It is *we* who need time to work through the new insights our renewing minds are discovering, for such insights, such new knowledge will radically change our whole stance or outlook on life. St Paul who went overboard and over the wall at Damascus after he first met the Lord, spent time in Arabia and back home in Tarsus where he would have worked through with the Lord the implications of what he now knew.

The Lord knows we need time to adjust and think and change. Yet, my growth, if I dare say such a thing, has happened because I have encountered the Lord several times over the years. These meetings are intermittent, for I am talking about when we *know* we are before Him face to face, when there is a deep and awesome coming together person to person. Such meetings are intermittent because we receive so much new insight and revelation in them that we need time between them to work through what they mean for us. I call those meetings with the Lord, 'baptism experiences'.

Baptism Experiences

As I mentioned above, when people are married, they ceremonially hand over their whole selves to their partner, but in the realities of marital life, they soon discover many areas which they have kept for themselves. When the right time has come, I have discovered that as I share these secret thoughts and feelings with my wife, and she her secrets with me, in ways we did not do before; when we have opened our hearts to each other at deeper levels than before, then so often we have a 'marriage experience'.

We feel there is a fresh unity between us. We move

closer to each other. So often these experiences draw out of us and refresh the emotions and feelings we had on our wedding day (the joy and love, I mean, not the nervousness!). Not surprisingly then, there is an extra delight in each other after one of these 'marriage experiences'.

What is happening is that these mutual self-disclosures are the process of making our proclaimed wedding-day unity become a reality in our lives. These disclosures are not intellectually cold things. When they happen, we are speaking about who we are from the depth of our being. Our hearts are open to each other; we stand naked and vulnerable. It is a meeting of each other in which our whole personality is involved, so besides communicating in words what we feel and are, our emotions, too, resurge and assert our joy and love for each other. Sometimes the sense of unity is so profound that it seems stronger than what we felt on our wedding day, but the truth is that all of *these experiences are rooted in and derive from our commitment to each other on that day*. So we do not doubt the sincerity of our wedding-day vows and rush off to church to be remarried every time we have a deep 'marriage experience'. We know these events are part of the process of becoming what we already are in God's sight.

'Baptism experiences' are akin to these 'marriage experiences'. They happen when we open our whole being, our whole self to the Lord. They occur when we hand over to Him the deepest part of our personalities, when we confess our hopes and joys, our sorrows, sins and fears. In other words, when we, as we would in any other deep relationship, expose ourselves in trust to Him who loves us. And it is at times like those we can so often receive fresh insights from the Lord and a rekindled love and joy. As the word 'experiences' suggests, especially if they are similar to marriage ones, they will and should happen more than once. And that is the truth. There will be many experiences of the Holy Spirit, in the same way as there will be many times and opportunities of giving more of ourselves to our partners or close friends.

In the New Testament, we hear of the Apostles being filled with the Holy Spirit ('baptism experiences') on at least two separate occasions. They were filled of course on the Day of Pentecost, but they were filled again as described in Acts 4:31. In that case, the Apostles had been hauled up before the Jewish authorities. It was only a matter of weeks beforehand that these same people had condemned the Lord Jesus to death. I wonder if Peter and his colleagues became conscious of their need to be bold. But he opens up that awareness in his life when he prays: 'And now Lord, look upon their threats, and grant to thy servants to speak thy word with all boldness . . .' (Acts 4:29). The Lord met him! 'And when they had prayed, the place in which they were gathered together was shaken, and they were all filled with the Holy Spirit and spoke the word of God with boldness' (v. 31).

St Paul also exhorted the Ephesians, 'be filled with the Spirit' (Eph. 5:18), which if translated more accurately would say, keep on being filled. Paul sees being filled with the Spirit as an ongoing process.

The times when we know we have met the Lord afresh, those events when our whole lives are filled again with new bursts of joy and love for the Lord, those occasions when we have new insight and a fresh zeal, those things I call 'baptism experiences'. Why 'baptism'? – because they are rooted in and derive from what Christ has already done for me when I was first united with Him.

I find there can be quite a lot of confusion in some Christian circles when people try and identify the time they actually received the Holy Spirit. Was it when they were converted? Was it when they were baptised in water? Was it when they were confirmed? Was it when they spoke in tongues? Doubtless there are other experiences of God you could add. The confusion resolves itself once we realise that when these experiences happen *after* our turning to Christ and acknowledging Him as Lord (a saving faith which in the New Testament was *immediately* followed by baptism in water), then they are 'baptism experiences'. Those wonderful times of knowing the Lord Jesus in a fresh and joyful way are rooted in and stem from what the Lord has *already* declared us to have and to be when we were first united with Him. Baptism is very similar to a wedding day, for it is the day when the Lord Jesus ceremonially unites the believer to Himself. As in marriage we hand over everything we are to our beloved, so too the believer hands over all of his or her life to the Lord Jesus, but the Lord Jesus also gives us everything that He is. St Paul writes, 'He is the source of your life in Christ Jesus, whom God made our wisdom, our righteousness and sanctification and redemption' (1 Cor. 1:30). The Lord is all of those things and He has given them all to us. That is why we have already received the Holy Spirit, because it is the Spirit of the Son of God. He has given His very self to us. That all happened when we were united with Christ. The Lord has not withheld anything from us. There is nothing He can add to what He has already given to us.

Yet, though in principle and in all sincerity, we gave ourselves totally to our Lord, we know that there will be many areas in our life which still have to come under His rule. So when I bring myself open-heartedly to my Lord, when perhaps I have discovered a part of me which is not under His lordship, when I confess those things and own up to what I am to Him; when I discover in Him great riches I never realised were there; when I look to Him for more of His love in my life; in other words whenever I let myself meet the Lord Jesus at an ever-deepening level of my being, so often it is then that my whole being experiences a fresh love for Him, and I feel I am united with Him. But these times are not our conversion or necessarily the time we receive His Spirit – they are 'baptism experiences' – experiences of Christ which are a working out in us what we have already received and are 'in Christ'. *These 'baptism experiences' are a fundamentally important part of the process of becoming what we are already in God's sight.* In fact, I would be so bold as to say that any relationship we have, be it with God or a human being, which avoids or lacks these sort of deep personal encounters, will inevitably grow stale and eventually wither.

Of course, these baptism experiences help us grow into *everything* we have from God, which includes 'the mind of Christ', but that gift cannot merely be one among lots of others. The mind of Christ is fundamental for us, because it gives us the sure foundation to thinking and perceiving in God-centred ways. Our desire is to be the same as our Lord's, and His desire was to do the will of His heavenly Father. God's will was His will in everything. No one can perceive the Kingdom of God unless they have the 'eyes to see and ears to hear'.

It would be quite wrong to think that these experiences with the Lord work by simultaneously moving the whole of our being nearer to what He has given us, like bringing a kettle of water to the boil. In other words, every time I meet God, I do not have a slight increase in my love, a slight increase in my wisdom, a slight increase in my holiness, a slight increase in a new mind . . . and so on. What happens is that when these experiences occur we may well move mightily forward in some areas of our life, but other areas may lie untouched by the Spirit for most of our lives. Someone once likened conversion to inviting the light of Jesus into a house in total darkness. We invite Him over the threshold into the dark house of our lives, and we are converted, but then we have *to invite Him* into each of the dark rooms and bring His light. So at any moment of time, our house will be a mixture of light where Christ has come and darkness where He has yet to go. I suppose you could equate Christ's entering into a darkened room of our lives with a 'baptism experience'. Well, the most important room in most houses is that which has an outside view, the room of our mind, and it is into that room we need to invite the Lord.

There is one obvious reason why we may not have

invited Christ into that particular area of our lives. We *did not know* we had to! I have discovered as I look back on my life, that *my ignorance about what God wants to do with me, has prevented me from asking Him to do it*. For example, even though I had been going to church for many years, I was ignorant of the truth that I could know the love and forgiveness of the Lord Jesus for *myself*. Naturally, I knew that in a general way, but I *did not know that I could know it personally*. Since I was ignorant of it, I did not go about looking for it. I missed out on God for far longer than I should, but it was my lack of knowledge that prevented me from asking Him to do that particular work in me. I suspect the same ignorance is at work in blocking out the so-called charismatic gifts of the Spirit. I have been told that some of these gifts have always been in the Church. Even in the darkest days of the Church's history, there were the few saints who spoke in tongues and healed the sick, but if most Christians were like me twenty years ago, we never sought the charismatic gifts because we simply did not know about them. It is not that so-called non-charismatics were second-class Christians, indeed many of them have a greater sense of God than some charismatics I have come across, rather it was an area in which they did not know the Lord could work.

So overcoming ignorance is more often than not the way to open doors through which the Holy Spirit can come.

Luther and Wesley in their day overcame ignorance with knowledge of how the Lord wanted to work in us. Luther overcame the ignorance of personal salvation in the mediaeval church by rediscovering that great New Testament truth, justification by faith. Yet, he did not merely discover a doctrine, he fell upon an insight, a revelation, which opened a door for the Holy Spirit to work that truth in himself and thousands of others. So, too, with John Wesley. The Moravians, who showed him the reality of personal assurance and the personal love of Jesus Christ, did not merely teach him a dogma, they revealed the way the Lord could work in him. He both learned and applied that lesson, and his great evangelistic efforts brought thousands of people into the same knowledge and experience of God.

This book will not have achieved its aim if it has merely shown you a few intellectual ideas about repentance. My purpose is to dispel ignorance of what repentance means so you will want to invite the Holy Spirit to work in your mind. In fact, my primary intention does not lie with the details of what I have said about repentance for I have no intention of writing correct doctrine for its own sake. I simply want to show you the truth that the Holy Spirit desires to renew our minds; He wants to move us closer to our goal of 'the mind of Christ in us'. The question we need to ask ourselves is: 'Do I have a renewed mind?' In other words, have I invited the Holy Spirit to come into the whole way that I respond and understand life and to change it so that I think the way Jesus did? Of course, we can answer that in a general sense for we can affirm that Christ's mind is in some way already in His people, but like the certainty of that knowledge of *personal salvation*, like the assurance that Jesus *loves me*, do we think, understand and live in it, in a way which assures us that we have renewed minds? There can be no doubt that if salvation has to be grasped personally and made our own, so, too, does repentance.

The text at the beginning of this chapter quoted part of St Paul's letter to the Ephesians. Why were the Gentiles alienated from the life of God? Because of *the ignorance* that is in them! But, brothers and sisters, you *did not so learn* Christ, so put off your old nature and *be renewed in the spirit of your minds*.

Our ignorance about renewal may be the most common reason why we may not have invited Christ's light into that room of our lives. It is when we know what we really are that we can invite the Holy Spirit to meet with us and do His work.

The mind-changing process is the means by which we

move closer to that mind of Christ we already have. The transformation will include two things:

a) *Baptism Experiences*
  — When we come to the Lord with all our difficulties in thinking His way;
  — when we begin to see yet another area of our minds which is in the grip of other ways of thinking; and
  — when we know we need fresh insight into God's ways in His world.

b) *Time*
  — to let what we have received work its way through our being;
  — to let our inner minds be changed and refashioned; and
  — to let ourselves put into practice the implications of new ways of thinking.

Of course we first have to recognise those parts of our mind which are in need of renewing. I am sure we should all readily admit that no one has a totally renewed mind, so how can we find out what dimensions of our thinking about God, the world and ourselves actually need to be changed?

It is worth looking once more at what happens in close relationships. Why is it that the 'honeymoon' period between newly-weds or good friends who share a house, comes to an end? It is because they are learning to live together. They are discovering each other's boundaries, sometimes through friction and argument. They are finding out what they are prepared to give of themselves to those around them and the others, too, are learning what they can expect of them. It can be a painful process.

A simple example with newly-weds would be where the husband expected to keep his salary and give his wife money for housekeeping. Her expectations might be very different! Those differences will have to be resolved, but they may not become apparent until the day comes when she asks for the cheque-book. There may be friction, a row, but they will then know where they stand. The conflict and arguments declare there is an unresolved difference between them, showing that a particular attitude about money has to be brought into the marriage.

If the difference in outlook on money is major and never resolved, it will leave a significant weakness in their relationship. It will be a specific area where one or the other refuses actually to be married. On the other hand, if the couple resolve the difference to the satisfaction of both, then their marriage or friendship will develop substantially. Disturbance and conflict can therefore produce growth because they declare to those involved where they truly are, and point to what they must resolve.

We are all used to handling personal discomfort, unpleasant as it sometimes is, and have our own experiences of relationships disintegrating, but we know many other situations of creative growth. Conflict and tension can tell us how much we have actually put ourselves into our relationships and consequently show us in what areas we can move forward. That is true in our relationship with husband, wife and friends; it is equally true in our relationship with the Lord Jesus. Once we have confessed Him as our Lord, setting our minds, He will begin to challenge the way we relate to Him.

Since the Lord desires us to have His mind in all things, He will help us to discover the boundaries of where we are in our thinking and responding to life by finding out what we *really* believe and how much we *actually expect* to recognise God in His world. He does that by disturbing us and making us uncomfortable. He will make demands on us, challenging us to identify those areas of our mind which need to be brought into our life with Him.

What are those disturbing forces, forces which could be painful and even frightening, forces which could be destructive or creative? They are 'doubt' and 'disbelief'.

7

CHALLENGING OUR MINDS

Doubt and Disbelief

I used to work for one of the companies in the soap and detergent industry. It was the days when biological washing powders were fashionable, and they occasionally advertised the superiority of their product by what I called 'miracle-tests'. One soiled shirt would be washed in ordinary detergent, and an identical one in biological washing powder. Stubborn stains were still visible in the one washed in ordinary detergent, but they had disappeared in the shirt washed in biological detergent. You were then supposed to be so impressed that you would buy a packet the next time you went shopping.

Now there is a 'miracle-test' for Christians, too. This test is obviously not about detergents, but rather about discovering what sort of mind you have and how you perceive and relate to the world around you.

So let me explain the miracle-test. It is quite simple. You *listen* to someone tell you about a God-given healing which has happened to them or someone else, and then *you feel how you respond to it*.

Alternatively, read some of the books describing the healings and raisings from the dead being experienced in other countries, and *watch how you are reacting* to reading those accounts.

Some years ago, just after my conversion, I sat at the feet of a local Church of England vicar, who shared many things with us including his experiences in the healing ministry. One story was about a wonderful miracle.

A young boy was running around the playground of his school, and ran between another boy and a wall, just as the other boy was throwing a dart. The dart went into the boy's eye. He was rushed off to hospital. The injury was very serious. The eye would have to be removed not only because it was so badly damaged, but because there was risk that infection would also harm the other eye. The boy's mother was a Christian and sent for this vicar to pray for healing for the boy. The vicar arrived to find the consultant talking to the boy's father, asking permission to operate at once. The father was an atheist. He listened to the consultant and the vicar and made his decision: 'I am going to let God have the first chance.' The boy was anointed for healing, his eyes were bandaged over. The next morning his eye was perfectly whole.

I discovered the power of the 'miracle-test' by telling that story to various people, and the extent of their reactions has been quite remarkable. Some have genuinely praised God for His work; most have smiled, kindly, but I knew they didn't really believe a word I was saying; and a few have become quite agitated. One even exploded and said: 'Was it ever reported to the British Medical Association?' I will readily admit that there is a mystery of why God acts here in this way and apparently not in the same way over there. You do not need the 'miracle-test' to show up that genuine difficulty! The test worked by revealing that those people simply did not believe a word I said to them. They probably thought me a gullible fool to take the story in, even dangerous if they thought I had invented the whole episode. At the best they would have thought it mistaken – the dart did not really go into his eye – the doctors made a wrong diagnosis – it all got rather exaggerated. The explanations are as numerous as there are hearers of the story.

What had happened? Their disbelief had kept what I told them at arm's length from them.

Of course, it is not a new problem. Jesus met the same wall of disbelief and doubt when He healed the sick. Just look again at some of the miracle stories to see how the religious authorities would not let themselves acknowledge who Jesus was. There is the story of the man born blind (John 9). The Lord made clay and anointed his eyes and sent him to wash in the pool of Siloam and his sight was restored. But look at those mind defence mechanisms at work.

> The neighbours and those who had seen him before as a beggar, said 'Is not this the man who used to sit and beg?' Some said, 'It is he'; others said, *'No, but he is like him'* (John 9:8–9; my italics).

Then, they took him to the religious authorities and told them all about the miracle.

'The Jews *did not believe that he had been blind* and had received his sight . . .' (v. 18; my italics). Reluctantly they agreed that something had happened after they had cross-examined the man's parents. Jesus did heal the sick, but by whose authority? They explained the Lord's power to heal by muttering that He had received it from Satan himself.

'He is possessed by Beelzebub, and by the prince of demons he casts out the demons' (Mark 3:22). I suppose that was their equivalent to our explaining miracles when we ascribe them to 'the power of the mind over matter'. They doubted who Jesus was, even if they acknowledged He had power over sickness and disease.

The miracle-test, whether it is healing signs, personal conversion, or any situation where God moves, will always sift our hearts and thoughts to see how we respond to the things of God.

If we are honest, how do we feel when someone tells us about some great miracle in their lives? I suspect that if you are like me, you may smile and say, 'Alleluia, praise the Lord', but haven't you at some time or other experienced a shrinking feeling inside, and a voice somewhere inside your head has said something like, 'Come on, tell us another!' I have had that experience and still do at times. It is disbelief and doubt.

But I want to emphasise that you need not be despondent about feeling doubtful. If we are prepared to acknowledge that we doubt, it can become a useful tool to help us grow spiritually. However, if we neglect it, it will fester inside us and make it hard for our minds to respond to what God is doing.

Doubt and disbelief are like fleas; it is not wrong to have them, but keeping them as they are will give us a very uncomfortable spiritual life.

Rescuing Doubt and Disbelief

So how do we rescue doubt? As I understand, from hearing about heart-transplant operations, our bodies have an in-built ability to detect the presence of a foreign organism. Once they detect its presence, they then work to isolate and expel what does not belong. That seems to be very essential for our health, after all if I get something in me, I want a body which 'knows' what to do to destroy such intrusions. Unfortunately our body defences cannot tell the difference between something which is for my good or something which would harm me. I am glad to know my bloodstream will work in such a way as to destroy foreign viruses in me, but I am not so happy to know that the same defences work to reject the new heart which I have been given in an operation. My body defences simply say, *'This thing is different'* and they consequently set out to isolate and destroy it.

I want to suggest to you that our minds, too, know how to protect themselves *as naturally* as our bodies do. Bodies have antibodies, *minds have doubt*. The purpose of doubt is in the first place to protect our minds. It works like our body defences by first of all *detecting difference*.

As we discovered in the first chapter, our minds are

formed to give us a particular way of understanding the world around, and doubt works to protect that understanding by keeping information at bay which is different. So, if our way of understanding excludes miracles, when we hear about one, or see one before our eyes, doubt will come flooding in to keep that information out. Doubt always comes into play where there is a difference between how we think things should be and what we may be hearing or seeing. In that sense, *doubt is a natural function of our minds*, and as such we should see it operating in all human beings in every realm of experience.

Galileo was convinced that the sun was at the centre of the solar system and the earth rotated around it. He had great difficulty in persuading both the religious and scientific authorities of his day! They doubted what he said because it was different from how they believed things were. Doubt works to detect difference.

However, *we fail to see* that like the antibodies in our bloodstream, *doubt only detects difference, doubt cannot decide on the truth or falsehood of the new information we are hearing or seeing*.

Our worst mistake is in assuming that the things we doubt must therefore be false, lies, deceptions or delusions. Certainly that is how doubt feels, but we must recognise that those feelings themselves are *only* a mind-response to difference. Those feelings have no capability to decide between what is good or bad for our minds. Indeed, in certain brain-washing conditions, I am sure our minds can be adjusted to take in, without any doubts at all, all sorts of grossly immoral and wicked ideas. Auschwitz is just one example of that.

We must separate that natural feeling of doubt – the shrinking-away feeling, the sense of disbelief, the looking down our nose, the 'tell us another one' – from trusting in our doubts as giving us a true judgment. We thank our doubts for detecting difference, but we shall be seriously handicapped if we trust their judgment on what is true or false. We must doubt the value of the judgment pronounced by our doubts.

Using Doubt for Growth

Now, if we can see that doubt works by detecting difference, and accepting the feelings doubt produces, then doubt can become a powerful tool for spiritual growth.

Let us take the example of the blind man that Jesus healed (John 9). The miracle-test generated doubt and disbelief. That was quite natural, after all, even today not many people born blind receive their sight. The ordinary people as well as the religious authorities had no previous experience of such things. Such a healing would have been an event as foreign to them as it would be to most of us. Their minds would not know how to cope with such an influx of amazing information. So what happens? The miracle occurs. The people saw the healed man returning, and immediately their minds generated doubt to isolate such an unusual event. So it is not at all surprising that some of them said, 'No, but it is like him.' Doubt has detected and isolated an event which was quite foreign to the way they usually understood the world around.

The onlookers now have two possible courses of action for dealing with their doubt. They can trust the judgments pronounced by their doubt and never acknowledge that a miracle happened, or they can use their doubt by seeing it delivers a challenge to their minds' capacity in understanding supernatural events.

The process then of using doubt to further our spiritual growth is first of all to acknowledge and accept those disbelieving responses as no more than natural reactions to something that is merely different to what our minds have previously experienced and understood. Doubt means that my mind is declaring, 'I do not know how to understand this. I have nothing to compare it with. This information is beyond my comprehension.' Simply recognise the difference that disbelief is revealing. Then we can ask ourselves, 'Why is there a difference?' and so begin the next stage of using our doubts for growth.

The *second part of the process* is to do with how we handle that acknowledged difference. Every so often, if you are like me, you have what we call 'a difference of opinion' with other people, which shows up in argument and conflict. We usually deal with these differences of opinion in one of two possible ways. We can maintain, despite all the evidence, that we are in the right and they are in the wrong. Or we can let the realisation dawn upon us that perhaps they were right in what they said after all, and we were wrong. Then we have to change our minds.

We need to handle the difference our doubt shows up in exactly the same way. We can dogmatically and doggedly maintain that we understand things just as they really are, and therefore miracles must be a hoax or a trick performed by deceivers; or with some humility we can look at the challenge of a reported healing sign to discover whether or not we might have to change our minds. Of course, this challenge to our minds by such use of doubt has a far wider application than in dealing with our problem over miracles. It can apply to every dimension of life, because doubt is a natural mind-defence to any alien information. The authorities who doubted Galileo's insights, for example, could have registered 'a difference of opinion', and instead of branding him a heretic, could have examined both the evidence and their own preconceptions to decide whose opinion was right. It is easy to say that today in that particular case; hindsight is perfect wisdom, but if they had used doubt creatively, *their understanding* of the relationship of the sun to the solar system would have changed. Of course, I am not saying we should swallow everything we hear, 'hook, line and sinker', indeed we should check as carefully as we can the truth of what is being told to us, which seems to have been the case with the man born blind. There was doubt initially when the blind man returned seeing. The crowd was confused as it tried to work out whether he was the same man or not. He proved that it was. 'I am the man!' Consequently, there could be no reasonable hesitation about what had happened to him. They then, accepting the truth of what they had seen and heard, would need to reflect on why they found it hard to accept that healing event.

The religious authorities, too, quite rightly, needed to make sure the healed man was not tricking them. They did not believe that he had been blind and received his sight until they had checked it with the man's parents. But once the truth of the story had been verified, then they should have let that event challenge the way their minds worked, demanding of them the real reasons why they disbelieved. It was their understanding that had to change.

It is exactly the same for us. The miracle-test happens. There has been a healing sign, a conversion story, someone has started speaking in tongues. How do we respond to those events? If, after careful examination, there are no *real* reasons for disbelieving then our doubts declare that we must attend to how our mind thinks about the world. It is our perceptions that need to change.

Once I used to feel guilty, even though I was the leader of a church, when folk came to me to tell me about great and minor miracles that had happened in their lives. I felt guilty because of my doubts, until I discovered the power of the 'miracle-test'. But now, I praise God for doubts, because I recognise that they reveal the frontiers of my expectations in seeing God at work. Doubt detects an area of faith discrepancy, a difference which will be resolved as I realise that my mind needs to be changed and reshaped to handle God-initiated events. So when someone tells me a story which I can see is true, if I am registering doubts, I recognise them, rejoice with the person over what they have told me, and go to God for Him to do some work in me.

How He does that reshaping and re-forming work on our minds is the subject of the next chapter, but we only grow when we see the need for our minds to be changed. Doubt challenges the mind, demanding that the way we see things may not be the way things really are.

I remember an occasion when doubt helped to bring an atheist doctor into a living faith in Jesus Christ. A couple of years before I really knew the doctor, he was working on the children's ward in the local hospital where I was chaplain.

It was four o'clock in the morning. The telephone rang. Would I come please to administer baptism to a four-year-old who was desperately ill with meningitis?

It was very serious. I went immediately to the ward where the child lay desperately ill. The medical staff left for a few minutes, and I administered baptism surrounded by the child's parents and grandparents. It did not take long. The staff wanted to return as soon as possible.

It needs no saying that the parents were very distressed. They knew their little girl was near to death. I remember saying to them, 'Let's just pray for a miracle,' and so we prayed tearfully and simply.

A week later the child was discharged from hospital in perfect health.

What I did not know at the time was that the attendant doctor was the atheist. As atheists believe there is no God, their mind perceives and understands the world never expecting to see God around. But what do you do when you see a child who was near to death recover to perfect health? Even an atheist's mind will register doubt – what has actually happened does not match with what an atheistic mind believes ought to happen.

I knew nothing of this until some two or three years later. I was visiting this doctor and his wife who had recently become Christians. There had been several strands in their conversion, but he asked me, 'Mike, does God heal without anyone praying?' I assumed a wise look, 'Well, I suppose He can, though I haven't really come across it. Have you anything in mind?'

He replied, 'A couple of years ago, there was a small girl in the children's ward desperately ill with meningitis. She was near to death, but a week later she walked out of hospital in perfect health, and I am absolutely convinced that our drugs did not cure her.'

I replied, 'Was her name . . . ?'

He sat bolt upright. 'Yes, but how did you know?'

This doctor experienced doubt. He saw something happen which his atheistic mind would not be able to understand. I am sure if there were other atheists on the staff that early morning, they could well have dismissed the healing event as 'spontaneous recovery'. It would not necessarily have challenged them at all. Yet this event challenged this doctor to examine his preconceptions. Doubt niggled away at his atheism. Every time he declared to himself 'God does not exist', his memory said, 'What about that little girl?' Eventually he was man enough to come to accept the truth of the situation. God, whoever He was, had indeed performed a miracle. But if God has done that, where does that leave one's atheism? This young doctor was being set up for a radical change of mind. Doubt had challenged it, the Lord God would soon change it.

8

EXPANDING OUR MIND'S FRONTIER

Jesus said, 'For truly, I say to you, if you have faith as a grain of mustard seed, you will say to this mountain, "Move from here to there," and it will move; and nothing will be impossible to you' (Matt. 17:20).

I was discouraged by that verse for many years because I totally misunderstood what it meant. I thought 'faith as a grain of mustard seed' meant my faith had only to be *as big as* a grain of mustard seed. Since mustard seeds are reputed to be the tiniest of all, then I only need a little bit of faith for mighty miracles to happen. Unfortunately, nothing happened at all! My faith, small as it was, could not even worry a molehill, never mind move a mountain.

Then I realised my mistake. The Lord did *not* say 'faith *as big as* a grain of mustard seed', He said 'faith *as* a grain of mustard seed'. What do mustard seeds do? Tiny as they are, they grow! '. . . it is the smallest of all seeds, but when it has grown it is the greatest of shrubs and becomes a tree' (Matt. 13:32).

Jesus was not teaching us about the quantity of faith we need, but the *type of faith* we must have – a faith, that though starting from small beginnings, grows to fill out the whole of our lives. Growth in faith means a growing expectation in seeing the Lord at work in us and in His creation. We do not believe in nothing, but in something definite and precise, and those 'somethings' as discussed in Chapter 2 are 'the things above'. Paul exhorted us to set our minds on them. The greater our faith, the more

we shall be set on those promises and on the Lord Jesus
Himself. The more 'those things above' grasp us and
shape our minds, the greater our faith will be that we
shall receive them.

The well-known verses from Hebrews 11:1–3 clearly
link faith, the things above and our understanding.

> Faith is the assurance of *things hoped for*, the conviction
> of things not seen. For by it the men of old received
> divine approval. By faith we *understand* that the world
> was created by the word of God (my italics).

Growing in faith and a mind growing into Christ's
ways of understanding the world are the head and tail of
the coin of our developing relationship with the Lord.

Yet, when I dare look back on my own growth in faith
and knowledge of what God does, I do not see my
growth as a steady, gradual upwards movement, like
climbing a hillside. I am not a little more faithful today
than I was this time last week. My faith growth has been
in jumps, more like climbing steps than going up a
gradual slope, but even then, the height and depth of the
steps have never been the same. It seems that for long
periods of my life I have remained at a particular level of
faith. I remained on that plateau until I was suddenly
pushed up on to a new level. Usually something has
happened, sometimes quite dramatically. Perhaps I have
been faced with important decisions, and then I find as I
look back that I have been pushed, pulled or kicked up on
to another level of faith.

Then I find the same process happening. I can stay on
that new level for some time until something else pushes
me up another stage.

It's a bit like jumping up the stairs, but staying for a
while on each step to catch your breath. Of course, this is
another way of thinking about baptism experiences (the
jumps) and the time needed to consolidate what has
happened to us (the levels).

The danger to growth is that we might be content to remain at a particular faith level and not take the risk of moving forward by taking step-jumps. That would then be like a marriage which would not take the risk of 'marriage experiences' – a sure recipe for staleness and eventual decay.

It can help, however, if we know which level of faith we are on; after all, most journeys start from where we know we are. We can discover where we are in our faith-growth by *discovering the boundaries* of what we *really* believe.

Now, I am sure that if I asked you if you believed God could do anything, you would with all sincerity say He could. But if you were put on the spot and asked to pray for healing for someone dying of cancer, how would you feel then? When we are pushed to our faith's limits, what do we *really* believe? We need to look at ourselves and become aware of ourselves so we can discover the areas where we have to grow. We apply the miracle-test I described in the last chapter. Do you recall how doubt and disbelief detect the difference between how we actually think about the world and what our minds are seeing and hearing? *Those areas where we register such doubts and disbeliefs are the boundaries of our faith.* Let me repeat what I said in that chapter about challenging our minds, I do not want us to feel guilty about natural doubt. It is the way our minds work. Consequently, doubt helps us to define our faith-boundaries, showing us which level we are on. But faith-boundaries show us the edges of our belief. We know where we are. We know the areas where we are anxious about our faith. Growth in faith happens when we face our faith-boundary uncertainties and doubts. Faith will stay on the same level if we avoid those edges and turn back from pushing them out.

Here are examples of some levels and faith-boundaries from my own experience. They are selective and, other than level B, are not in any order of spiritual importance except that this is how it happened to me.

Please do not be put off by what looks to be an

emphasis on the supernatural. I have chosen them because they are *simple illustrations*, in that it is easy to recognise immediately the effect of changing from one level to another.

In fact, my transition from being just a 'prayer-talker', banging on the doors of heaven with my incessant words, to a 'praying-listener' on Level C, has been for me the most important change of levels, after conversion. It was only a beginning and it could indeed have its own series of levels and jumps.

The next chapter develops how we can use meditation and waiting on the Lord to further our growth. This chapter describes *how* we can move from any type of faith and knowledge level to another, be that supernatural, meditative or a more Christ-centred way of looking at the world.

	Activity	Faith-Boundary
Level A	Going to church	Can I really know Christ personally?
Level B	Converted to Christ	What's the point in spending so much time in quiet prayer?
Level C	Being still with God	I really can't see the purpose of speaking in tongues.
Level D	Charismatic gifts	I feel very sceptical when people tell me about miracles.
Level E	Healing of the sick	Come on! Who believes in the devil, anyway?
Level F	Spiritual warfare	Raise the dead! You must be joking!

The activities represent what faith-level I was on. Each line represents a faith-boundary that had to be crossed before I could reach the next level. From the side, this chart would look like this:

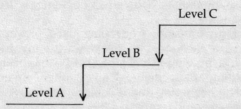

These diagrams show what sort of doubts I had. So I openly confess that I experience doubt and disbelief when I hear the stories of the dead being raised in the Philippines. It is my faith-boundary. I need to be taken through it so I can minister in that area, but at the moment that is where I am. Please God, there is much more to my spiritual life than these levels, but can you see how easy it is to remain on one level for the rest of your life? I have to say with a heavy heart that I know many people who are still at Level A, they are content with just going to church. When the Gospel is preached, calling them to make their decision for Christ, they do not or refuse to hear and thus avoid facing their faith-boundary. *The boundary is about uncertainty, it is about discomfort.* We can move away from it back on to the quiet plateau of a given level, or we can face our edges and grow through them. Of course, what applies at Level A, also applies at all the other levels. We can become content and spiritually inert at all levels of growth. No matter which level we believe we are on, the Lord is always calling us to go forward and become what we are. However, to do that we must go through our faith's boundaries.

Going through Boundaries

How can we change from one stage of faith to another? Let us take learning to swim as an example. There are two definite levels, people who are happy walking around on firm ground, and the next level where some of those people are happy swimming around in water. There is a definite boundary between the two stages. You can either swim or you cannot. Now how do people learn to swim, how do they move from one level to the other? They could have just been *dropped in* the water when they were babies, when they are supposed to swim instinctively. Most of us, however, have to learn patiently and laboriously. Yet some of us who learned this way have had to cope with doubts and fears about swimming. Our fears have told us our limits, they have informed us that we cannot swim. These doubts and fears define our boundaries, telling us just where we are. Yet, if we listen to these doubts and move away from them back on to firm ground, we shall never learn to swim. We have to go through these boundaries on to the next level.

Our growth to becoming what we are involves us moving from one level of faith to another through the boundaries of what we doubt, disbelieve and sometimes fear. There is a distinctive shift between faith-levels, as definite as the difference between being able to swim or not. However, the jumps necessary to take us from one level to the next are not something we can do by ourselves. *We can only go as far as standing on the edge of our level of faith acknowledging our doubts and fears. It is the Holy Spirit who alone can lift us up on the next level by a baptism experience.* He will meet with us if we are standing in the right place, desiring to grow in faith and knowledge.

In my experience, God helps us over the faith-boundaries using the ways we learn to swim; He drops us in the deep end, or He teaches us patiently and laboriously as He launches us into deeper encounters with Himself.

I shall now explain in detail three sorts of experience from the chart which show in a simple way the levels of my own growth in ministry. The stories are not spectacular, and I have chosen them because of that, for I do not want you to respond to the stories as stories, but rather to understand what spiritual processes were happening, to see, if you like, how the Lord taught me to swim at other levels of ministry.

I shall describe a 'dropped-in' experience, in which without any preparation at all, I was thrown into the deep end and had to learn from the Lord there and then.

I shall describe a change of level of ministry in which I was practising swimming on dry ground, and then was dropped into the water.

I shall describe how my faith-levels were changed by a patient and gradual slipping into the water until the day came when I was able to minister at a new level.

A Dropped-in Experience

I picked up the telephone. A man's voice spoke. He was hesitant, cautious. 'Is that the minister at the church?' I said it was.

He continued, 'Please do not think this is a joke. I am very serious. I have telephoned several other ministers and they have refused to come. Will you please take seriously what I am going to say?'

'Of course,' I replied. 'What's the problem?'

'My house is haunted. My daughter is seeing a ghost and this ghost is interfering with her small baby.' He went on to describe in detail what was apparently happening.

I can assure you, when all this happened to me many years ago, I could well understand why many of the local clergy had considered this man's story a hoax.

'Ghosts?' I thought. 'Ghosts? Who believes in such things these days?'

Yet the man seemed genuine in what he had said, and I had promised to take him seriously. So I decided to go round to his house as my pastoral duty. That sounds very cool and calm, but as soon as I had put down the telephone, I realised I was getting out of my depth. This was something, if real, I had never come across before. No one, but no one, thought seriously about the existence of ghosts. They certainly had no part in the way I thought about the world, and I can assure you that they were never part of my training at college. Here was something I had never come across, never thought about, except perhaps as a laugh over camp-fires as a Boy Scout. I had just been firmly placed in my faith-boundary about the possibility of other spiritual beings and forces than ourselves. I could have gone and dismissed all their fancies as flights of the imagination. I could have given them the benefit of my amateurish psychotherapy. I could have avoided it. But I knew I had to 'see' what was there.

I have never prayed so hard in my life as when I walked to their house. Now strange things happened to me when I was ministering to them. I heard their story and they told me what had been happening. There was no evidence of hoax, manipulation or psychological disturbance. Then, as I stood up to minister, I was bathed in a sense of total authority. I simply *knew* what I had to do, and what I had to say and what sort of spirit it was that I was dealing with. It was an experience similar to what happens when we say we 'rise to the occasion', finding ourselves doing or saying something far greater than we ever imagined we could.

Yet it was not I who rose to the occasion, but the Holy Spirit who took me up on to another level of knowing the Lord. At once, I realised I was not dealing with a poltergeist, an evil spirit or anything like that. It was the troubled soul of someone who had died. I knew that as clearly as knowing $2 + 2 = 4$. It was, I suppose, what some call the 'gift of knowledge'.

A verse came tumbling into my mind. 'For to this end Christ died and lived again, that he might be Lord both of the dead and of the living' (Rom. 14:9). I therefore prayed, and asserted the Lord's authority over the troubled soul, and in Christ's name, broke the ties which held it to that house. Peace came and remained.

God had thrown me in the deep end and granted me His knowledge and wisdom in that situation. It was a baptism experience. I knew I was helpless in that situation, I had confessed it and asked for Him to come, and He had met me, giving me all that I needed at that time. It was a faith and knowledge jump.

I appreciate that some of you might find that story totally bizarre and alien to anything you have ever experienced, and so would I have done some years ago. I could have responded like the other ministers in town and simply not have let myself become involved, but I suspect I would then have *kept myself away* from that particular sort of ministry. Yet, out of a sense of duty, God led me to stand in the midst of all my doubt and anxiety about the reality of the so-called supernatural. If you like, I had let myself go to my faith-boundaries, to *areas where I knew I could not cope and where I knew I would need the Lord to help me*. Moving into our faith-boundaries, moving to our limits, means we are going into areas over which we have little personal control. *It is there that we know we have to trust God to meet with us*. The Lord met me as I launched out to minister in His name. Even today I wonder how 'on earth' I knew what I had to do so the Spirit could bring peace into that household. He took me up to a new level in my ministry. But *another lesson* I learnt was that this new ministry experience and that influx of knowledge did not disappear when I returned home. That influx of knowledge took me up to a different level of understanding the mind of God and perceiving *everything* He has made, things both 'visible and invisible'.

Once you have personally experienced one of these level jumps, you do not have much mental difficulty in adjusting your outlook on life to make room in your minds for them. *Such new experiences and knowledge become 'food for thought'. After the event, our minds will spend time*

*examining and readjusting as they work out the implications
of what has happened.*

Let me point out to you a well-known phenomenon in
the healing ministry. It seems that the best healers, in the
sense that they are apparently used more than others in
bringing wholeness to others, are those who have been
healed themselves. A seriously ill person has been
brought for prayer. They let themselves be pushed forward towards the front for healing prayer. How often
they must be full of apprehensions and doubts as well as
a degree of hope. It is their hope which makes them stand
in the midst of their wondering whether God heals or
not. They are on their 'faith-boundary'. Then, by God's
mercy, the Holy Spirit meets with them and they are
instantly healed. By the nature of what has just happened they could not go back to their former faith-level
which doubted healing! They *know* it happens because
they have experienced the Lord doing it. It is a baptism
experience which lifts them on to another level.

Those who have been healed will probably spend time
examining and readjusting their outlook on miracles, but
will they not be full of faith in the God who heals? Of
course they will. It is those who are on that faith-level
whom the Lord can use far more easily than those who
are hesitant.

There are, of course, all sorts of examples of such
dropped-in faith-jumps at all levels. Think about the ones
you have experienced and how it has formed a new
outlook of mind in you.

A Prepared but Dropped-in Experience

When people are asked in charismatic circles which gift
they would like, they often reply that they would like the
gift of healing. I was among them. Yet I had a faith-
boundary. Every time someone told me with stars in their
eyes that they had been healed of something or other, I

felt a shrinking-away inside me which told me that I did not believe what they were saying. The miracle-test showed me the edges of my faith. If I wanted to move into the healing level of ministry, I would need to have a faith-jump through those doubts and disbeliefs.

So what do you do about it? We start by *preparing for ministry*, we apply to ourselves everything we learnt in Chapters 2 and 3. First of all, we come to the Lord, *setting our minds* on Him or the things above. Second, we come to Him, *confessing* He is Lord and owning up to what we are.

Let us look at how I practically *set my mind on the healing ministry*. The first thing was to see what Jesus did, to try and work out why He performed healings. That involved good old-fashioned Bible study.

> All scripture is inspired by God and profitable for teaching, for reproof, for correction, and for training in righteousness, that the man of God may be complete, equipped for every good work (2 Tim. 3:16–17).

If I wanted to inform my mind about the validity and necessity of the healing ministry, I had to examine the Lord Jesus's ministry and discover why signs and wonders were such an important aspect of His work. As far as I was concerned, not only did I have to work through a mind formed by the forces of this world, but also formed falsely by misinformation, because I had been taught at university that Jesus did not do miracles. I was taught that the Gospel writers put them in to glamorise the Lord so that the pagans would admit that He was the Son of God. Well, we each have a particular battle for our minds, but mine would only be resolved as I studied and prayed over what the New Testament said. In the end, I realised that everything Jesus did and said pointed to the coming rule of God, His Kingdom, when death and disease would no longer exist. I do not think that was merely an intellectual discovery, but it was also a gradual heart realisation as I prayed over what I was reading.

I must also say that in my case this study took a long time, possibly because of my initial intellectual handicaps. Then, as I grew more and more convinced about the factuality of the Lord's ministry, I dared to read 'sensible' testimony stories. I was very cautious! I was not going to read any cranky books, so I chose books written by thinking, reflective people whom I felt I could trust – men and women who would not let their enthusiasm and emotions take over their heads. What was I doing? I was making sure my information was sound and trustworthy. I talked to people who had been to healing services. I spoke to ministers who ran healing services. I did everything to validate the possibility of healing signs for today. I prayed over it, and slowly but surely I embraced the possibility that the Lord *could and would* heal today. I became content in my mind about that. It was something He could do through me if He wished. But I still had not been used. I suppose at the worst, I had submitted my mind to the possibility of miracles, and at the best, I now had a theology of healing even though I had no personal experience of it. And that is how it remained with me for two or more years. No one asked me to pray for healing for them, and I was not confident enough to go out and find my first victim. However, I had prepared myself as much as was humanly possible. I was right in the corner of my step ready to be pushed up to the next level. I was swimming on dry ground.

Then I was *dropped-in*. Again, the telephone rang.

'Hello, Mike. Gordon had a heart attack this morning. It is a mild one. The Lord says that you have to come over here and pray for Gordon's healing.'

This is when you start acclaiming the lordship of Jesus with all of your being, confessing Jesus is Lord and admitting that you have no competence to heal anyone. I was pushed in and my feelings and responses were exactly parallel to what I have explained when I was dropped into the 'supernatural' ministry. Yet the Lord met with us and Gordon was healed. I then *knew* for myself the reality of Jesus's healing work. He took me up on to the next level of ministry. I suppose I could echo what Job said when he met God: 'I had heard of thee by the hearing of the ear, but now my eye sees thee' (Job 42:5).

Beforehand I had an intellectual knowledge, afterwards I had a knowledge of healing based in experience. However, my preparations through study and finding out from others had helped me to accept the possibility of what the Lord could and would do. My mind had been softened up, even shaped, by what I had discovered in the Scriptures and from experienced Christian healers, but true knowledge came when I was myself used in the healing ministry. The Lord met with me. It was a baptism experience, an event created by the Spirit, which my mind has now had to integrate into its way of thinking not just about the possibility of miracles, but inevitably about the more important relationship between this creation and God's activity in it. Once we know miracles do happen, we cannot, if we work it through, believe God is so outside the world's structures that He is unable to be involved in them. When we permit the Lord to work in our minds regarding miracles, more happens than merely coming to a belief that His power is available today.

Perhaps one of the best examples of this sort of breakthrough of faith barriers is the story of the two disciples walking to Emmaus. The story is told in Luke 24:13–32. They initially saw all the events that had happened on one particular level of faith, for at the start they did not recognise the risen Lord, 'their eyes were kept from recognising him' (v. 16). With heavy hearts, they told the stranger all their hopes and aspirations about Jesus of Nazareth. They had even heard a report from some women who said He was alive. Can you see how these

two men were functioning on one level of faith? They had
heard about the Resurrection, they may even have believed there was something in it, but they were not on a
faith-level which *knew* it had really happened. So what
did Jesus do? He prepared them by using the Old Testament. 'And beginning with Moses and all the prophets,
he interpreted to them in all the scriptures the things
concerning himself' (v. 27). *Then* came the recognition
through the breaking of bread. 'And their eyes were
opened and they recognised him' (v. 31).

It was a baptism experience. The Lord had dropped-in
and lifted them up to another level of faith. Then they
saw and knew what had been happening to them, they
knew the answer as to why their hearts had been burning
in them. Nightfall or not, they went straight back to
Jerusalem to declare what had happened to them in the
breaking of the bread. They would never be the same
again.

A Prepared Way of Moving to the Next Level

I think it is true to say that, unlike many others, I never
had any doubts that the gift of speaking in tongues
should not be bestowed to the present-day Church, but
I did not have the gift. So I went through the sort of
preparation process I have just written about. I read the
relevant parts of the New Testament; I read the books
about the Charismatic movement which were beginning
to be published; I also talked at length with Pentecostal
friends and attended some of their services. I was trying
to discover what this gift was all about. Eventually, and
intellectually, I saw it could and did happen, but I had
one block in my mind. I simply could not see *why* God
should give it. I knew about its use for praise and
messages, but that did not really satisfy me. After all,
what is so wrong with praising God in English? I needed
to know why. Then one evening, Michael Harper came to

visit my theological college. In those days, Michael was a well-known apostle for the Renewal movement, and our common room had invited him to come and speak to us. I thought the meeting was quite cool, almost prickly, because for most of us what he said was as alien as if he had just arrived from Mars. He was operating on a different level from us, so there was no way most of my colleagues *could* see Christian ministry as he did. However, someone asked him, 'Why should God give the gift of speaking in tongues?'

Michael said, 'I was brought up in the sort of Protestant tradition which regarded Roman Catholics as almost, if not actually, the devil's seed. I would never dream of going near them, never mind pray with them. Then I was filled with the Spirit, I spoke in tongues, and now I see Roman Catholics as brothers and sisters in Christ, and I pray with Catholics quite often.'

Well, I suppose that answer didn't really impress my fellow students, but it gave me the answer to my question. The reason why God grants speaking in tongues is to help us *love*.

Thus my preparation for this gifting was a mixture of my search and God's revelation through someone who was experienced. I was now convinced that God would give it to me. I was at the foot of a step, ready for the spiritual jump. Yet preparation in itself was not enough. I had to learn something about *confession* – confession which realises who the Lord is and who I am before Him.

Now someone had told me 'how to start speaking in tongues'. What I had to do, they said, was to go somewhere quiet, pray for a while, bring yourself before the Lord and start making sort of nonsense sounds with your mouth – I suppose a sort of limbering up – and ask the Holy Spirit to come. I did this many times, but nothing happened, except that I felt more and more foolish. One day, I went through all the ritual, all the rigmarole, gobbled a few sounds. Nothing happened. Except – something inside my head clicked – a wheel turned – the light dawned – an explosive thought filtered into my conscious mind: '*You* cannot do this, only God can.' It was a confession from deep within me. Perhaps it was the voice of the Lord Himself, but I was immediately catapulted up into meeting Him. I had a baptism experience. I spoke in tongues and knew in my being the joy and love there are when He is with us. The Holy Spirit took me up to a new level of knowing Him. Such encounters can never be merely emotional experiences, but by necessity create an enriched or even different way of perceiving and understanding what the Lord does and how He works.

I have, of course, taken fairly simple examples of my own development in ministry. I sympathise with those who find such small examples somewhat tiresome. However, my desire is not to show you the details of my growth, but to take these simple examples to *reveal the process* by which the Holy Spirit has met with me and taken me up to further levels. Obviously, the particular way one individual is moved to another level may not be the same way that it happened to me. For example, my gifting with tongues was a 'prepared event'; the first disciples were gifted by a 'prepared, dropped-in event'; the believers in Caesarea by a totally unexpected 'dropped-in event', but the result was the same in each case.

I believe *all* growth in our love and knowledge of God comes about through this step-by-step process. We progress at any level when we are prepared or are taken into the boundaries of our faith where we work with the Lord on our doubts and disbeliefs, waiting for Him to meet with us. But if we avoid those edges, if we prefer to live on the plateau, keeping away from the anxiety of our boundaries of doubt, desiring the comfort of the safety of sure and certain places, then we shall never grow. We can only grow at faith's boundaries. That is what our faith teaches us about the Lord Jesus. When He went to the cross, He was in the depths of His doubts and despair.

He sweated great drops of blood in the Garden of Gethsemane. He knew the devastating pain of being abandoned by His Father. He hung there on the cross at the edge of His faith, waiting for the Holy Spirit to raise Him to the new heights of the glorious Resurrection. There is an old song which goes, 'If you will not bear a cross, you can't wear a crown'.

Let me summarise the process.

One   We must move to the edges of what we know.

Two   We move there by *studying and praying* through *what the Bible teaches*.

Three   We prepare by studying and discovering from those who claim to be putting into practice what we desire.

Four   The preparations are not the new levels of faith. They are one of the ways we 'present ourselves to Him as living sacrifices'.

Five   We wait on Him *as Lord* to come.

Six   The Holy Spirit meets us and takes us to the next level.

Seven   Our minds adjust to take in these new experiences. So often when we have reached a new level, we look back to why we did not see the things we see now. They were always there before, but our minds were blind to responding to whatever it was we now see.

9

MINDS MEETING GOD

In the last chapter we looked at the overall process how the Holy Spirit takes us up from one level of faith and knowledge to another. In this chapter, I want to examine in more detail how we may prepare ourselves to wait on the Holy Spirit to come to us, always remembering of course that He blows where He wills. The following diagram might help you to show the area we are now concerned with.

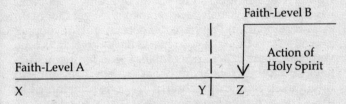

X to Z is the level of faith and knowledge we have now.

X to Y is the area where we are comfortable in that faith.

Y to Z is our faith's boundary, where we are anxious about what level B demands, and experience doubt and disbelief.

Z is the place where we meet with the Holy Spirit who takes us up to the next level of faith.

The last chapter gave some suggestions as to how through Bible-study and talking to others, we can move from point Y to point Z; this chapter is about how we remain at point Z and what we do as we wait for the Holy Spirit to come from on high.

So what are we waiting for at point Z? A baptism experience! We are waiting and praying to meet the Lord at a deeper level of our being. We are waiting on Him to make us become a little more of what we are already in Him.

I want us then to explore in greater depth what is involved in such baptism experiences by looking again at Jesus's baptism in the River Jordan. However, though I hope you will understand what I have written with your intellect, I want you rather to discover with *your whole self* what these baptism experiences are. This will involve us in doing two things: first, reading and understanding; second, using your imagination, emotions and will.

I am not suggesting we use our imagination to feel what is happening in baptism experiences just for the sake of it, I am suggesting it because I have discovered that a right use of our imagination can be a powerful means of directing how we think and behave in the 'real world'. For example, all of you at one time or another have probably quarrelled with someone, or got caught up in an argument, and perhaps did not account for yourself as well as you thought you should have done. If like me you have some experience of that, I wonder if you, too, have lain in bed rehearsing what actually went on; but this time, in your imagination, it has gone something like this: 'The next time John Smith says that to me, I will say this to him.' In other words we work through the past in our imagination so that when next time comes we shall know what to do. So, when we lie in bed our imaginations are not merely putting aside our anxiety over our poor performance, but also directing us to a more effective way of coping with the next difficult situation. Consequently, when I suggest we need to learn to use our imagination to understand what happens in baptism experience, although we may 'feel' what it is all about, a proper use of our imagination will also direct us to a more effective way of directing our lives. Some people call this active use of our imagination, meditation. Christians use meditation as a time of quiet when they ponder and dwell on what the Lord has done for them so that they can discover what He wants of them.

Returning then to think how we remain at point Z and come to a deeper understanding about baptism experiences, what I want you to do is to meditate upon the story of the Lord's baptism in the River Jordan. The story is recorded in Matthew 3:13–17. First of all, read it several times to discover the action and vividness of the event. The Lord *went into* the river. John *tried to stop* Jesus. Jesus *was baptised* (was He dipped, or was the water poured over His head?). The Spirit *came down* from heaven as a dove. There was *a voice* saying, 'This is my beloved Son, with whom I am well pleased.' I have italicised those words because they are either *words of action* or *words which portray relationship* between John and Jesus, or Jesus and the Father. What we are going to do is to visualise the action and put ourselves into the feeling of relationship. We are going to ask ourselves why John tried to stop Jesus, what did he feel in his heart, what did Jesus feel like when He submitted Himself to baptism?

Read the story a few times to make yourself familiar with the actions and the relationships. When you have done that we have to prepare ourselves to ponder and dwell on what the story means. Our aim is to use our imagination to 'see and feel' what happened to the Lord and how it can help us. What we shall do in the following exercises is to make ourselves and our intellectual, analytical skills become still and quiet so that the most fragile and sensitive parts of our minds – our imagination and feelings – may become active. We want to see what *they* can teach us. To do that we need to find somewhere relatively peaceful, since we need to become still and attentive to our imagination. Once you have found a bit of peace and quiet, here are a few tips to help you relax.

1. Sit comfortably on a straight-backed chair. Sit up straight with your legs uncrossed, feet flat on the floor

slightly apart. Close your eyes if you think you might be distracted.

2. Relax your body. You can do this by focusing your attention on your feet (I do not mean you look at them). You let yourself be aware of the sensations your brain registers from your feet – their weight on the floor, warmth, and so on. Do not analyse these sensations, simply let them be in your mind. Then you focus your attention in the same way on your legs, keeping in mind the sensations from your feet. Once you are aware of your feet and legs, continue by moving to your thighs, back, shoulders, arms and hands. The skill is in letting your mind become aware of all the sensations of your body – heaviness, lightness, the touch of clothes, etc. Keep practising this. It is only a skill. Keep going round your body until your limbs feel quite heavy, when it seems it would need quite an effort to lift your hand.

3. Focus your attention on to your face. Be aware of what your left cheek is feeling, then your right. Choose any part of your face. Keep on doing it. You are learning to be still but alert.

4. Focus your attention on to your nostrils and be aware of the coolness of the air you are inhaling, and the warmth of what you breathe out. This might take you some time and practice. Breathe quite deeply. The Greek word for spirit and breath is the same, so in a way when we breathe in fresh air, we are also inviting the Spirit of God into the deepest part of our being.

(It will take a little time to become experienced in all of that, but it becomes easier the more you practise. It is a skill which is very similar to that which pregnant women are taught about relaxation.)

The next stage is to give our imagination food for thought. Since our desire is to discover something of the inner meaning of Jesus's baptism, we start using our imagination to dwell upon that story. This is what you can do *in your mind's eye* when you are still:

SEE the River Jordan. See the colours of the flowers.
  Look at the distant hills. Watch the birds flying from
  tree to tree. There – the children are splashing around
  in the water.
HEAR the river breaking over stones and rocks. Notice
  the bird-song – can you hear that song-thrush? Hear
  the rustle of breeze in the trees – and the squeals of
  delight from the children at the water's edge.
FEEL the cool of the river in your hands. Touch the
  softness of the moss on the bank-side. Roll one of
  those pebbles around your fingers and feel its cool
  smoothness.

In other words, I am encouraging you to use your
whole self in your imagination. We do not understand
the world with our intellects, but with our whole being.
This sort of imagination states that everything about our
body is important in discovering the truth about life.
Therefore, use your whole self, sometimes as the ob-
server, sometimes as someone who is involved in the
picture. It is like constructing your own dream. Use your
own ideas of 'seeing' the River Jordan besides those I
have suggested.

The scene is now set. Let us move to the action. 'See'
John the Baptist up to his waist in the river. He is
baptising all those who come to him. Look at the crowd
on the river-bank as they wait to come to him. They look
solemn. It is quiet. They are conscious of their sins. In
their hearts they are wondering whether he is the promised Christ. Let yourself be aware of your own sins. Let
yourself be aware of your own need of forgiveness. Feel
the awe and fear when you hear John proclaim 'Repent
for the kingdom of God is at hand'. You are glad to be
there with all those others, glad for the opportunity to be
prepared for the coming of God.

Dwell in all of those feelings. When you are ready, look
in front of you in your meditation picture. There, just a
few people ahead, is Jesus of Nazareth. You did not

notice Him before, but there He is. Let your picture of Jesus come into your imaginary picture. Look at Him, identify with Him. He, too, is quiet and solemn. He, too, seems to know something of exceptional importance is happening. Try and feel what the Lord is feeling.

Perhaps Jesus, realising the waiting and preparation period is over, brims over with expectation and anticipation for His future ministry. It is time to begin His Father's work. It is graduation day. It is decision day. Jesus is experiencing the most momentous day of His life.

What did you feel like when you faced the most important day of your life? Perhaps like you and me, the Lord experiences several emotions. He might be a little anxious, conscious of His need for the Holy Spirit to come and equip Him for His work. Ask yourself why Jesus might feel He needs the Spirit. Is it because He already knows that He will need strength to endure the criticism and rejection of His own people? Is the shadow of Calvary's cross already on His mind? Yet, despite such possible fears and anxieties, the Lord knows the time is fulfilled. The day of salvation has come! God's rule is going to break out into His world through His ministry. There is a Gospel to bring to people. There is good news for the poor, the sick, the outcast and the sinner. Jesus comes to baptism, knowing He is not only the herald of good news, but embodies the contents of the Gospel. God's Son resolutely and determinedly commits Himself to bringing the Kingdom of God. He dedicates Himself to wrestling and overcoming the powers of Satan. Ponder and dwell on what the Lord might be feeling as He presents Himself to His Father to be commissioned for service. Do not try and think it out, rather let yourself be united with Jesus, and become aware of what your being is telling you about how the Lord might be feeling. Try and sense His anticipation and expectation.

Keep bringing the Lord Jesus into your imagined picture. Exercise your imagination. Now see Him as He comes close to John the Baptist. Feel the cool of the Jordan water as He wades in. Catch that moment of recognition as John looks up into Jesus's face. Feel the heart jump! This is no mere meeting with a long-lost cousin, this is an encounter with the promised king.

Now listen to why John the Baptist protested:

'No Jesus, no!'

'I need to be baptised by you and do you come to me?'

Do you 'see' why John responded in this way? Imagine how you would feel if you opened your front door and there on your doorstep stood the Queen of England or the President of the United States. You would be totally amazed that they had come to you. No wonder John tried to stop Jesus, because he recognised who He was.

But try now and capture what all of this is showing us about the Lord Himself. He knows who He is, yet He also knows His position before His heavenly Father. He is the obedient Son, who, as He will declare in His ministry, only does what He sees His Father is doing. The Lord Jesus approaches John knowing He, too, needs to be submissive to God His Father. Jesus knows who God is, but He also knows what God requires of every human being. *Jesus then comes out of a loving, submissive obedience to His heavenly Father.* The Lord had no need to confess His sins, yet this loving act of submission is His confession, for by submitting Himself to baptism, Jesus declares His dependence on His Heavenly Father.

So ponder on why the Lord replies to John, 'Let it be so now; for thus it is fitting for us to fulfil all righteousness' (Matt. 3:15), and see if you can become aware of Jesus's profound *humility* – a humility described in Philippians 2:7–8.

. . . emptied himself, taking the form of a servant, being born in the likeness of men. And being found in human form he humbled himself and became obedient unto death . . .

As the Lord Jesus stands before John waiting for baptism, I want you to capture *those two important feelings* in your imagination. *I want you to capture something of the Lord's humility in expressing His need of the Holy Spirit. I want you to capture at the same time His expectation and anticipation that the Spirit would surely come upon Him.*

In your mind's eye, see the Lord waiting. Catch that humble, expectant attendance on God. Let yourself be aware of the stillness and that sense that something of great importance is going to happen very, very soon.

The 'feeling' I want you to know is akin to what we experience when we are waiting for guests to come to dinner. We have spent most of the day preparing and cooking the meal, but it is now ready. The table is laid, the house prepared, the children are in bed fast asleep, and we are seated 'relaxing' for a couple of minutes as we wait for the doorbell to ring, informing us that our guests have arrived. The 'feeling' I want you to register is when we are 'relaxing' and waiting for the doorbell.

Let yourself be aware of that sort of experience as you ponder on how the Lord might be feeling as He waited under John's hand to receive baptism.

The Lord waits, prepared, humble and expectant. There is a deep stillness and a heartfelt desire to receive the Holy Spirit. Let yourself dwell there with Him, so you can experience something of what He might be feeling as He waited on His Father.

'Feel' what it is like. Be aware of what your whole being is telling you. Keep on coming back to this single moment so you know deep within you what was going on. It is important to find out.

It is important because the Lord Jesus is standing at point Z on His faith-level. He is at the point on any faith-level where we *all* need to be to receive the Holy Spirit. So when we let ourselves be aware of what happened to the Lord, *we are discovering how we ourselves are to stand at the edge of our faith and wait on the coming of the Spirit.*

It is no good teaching you that you must be humble, prepared and expectant upon God like Jesus, because such instruction is useless until you find out for yourself how *you* can and are able to stand before God. The meditation on Jesus's baptism can help you to do that, so I emphasise that the purpose of the meditation is not to learn how to meditate, but to help you discover with your whole being what it is for you to be humble, prepared and expectant before God. The meditation is only a tool to achieve that aim. Self-discovery is what is important. I am not interested in imparting knowledge only to your minds, rather I want you to have *experiential* knowledge.

The Lord Jesus then, shows us what it is like to stand at point Z on our faith-level, and demonstrates to us *how* we are to stand there in humble expectation. I exhort you to practise the meditation until you begin to know what it is like to wait like Jesus on the Holy Spirit. But you will not always receive baptism experiences of the Spirit, for not only does He blow where He wills, but as I have written previously, God will not take us up to new levels of faith and knowledge until we have had sufficient time to integrate the insights of the level we are on at present. Like our Lord Jesus, our time, too, has to be fulfilled. Nevertheless, as we can only catch a train from a railway station, so, too, if we are preparing to meet the Holy Spirit, we shall only meet Him when we have learned to wait humbly and expectantly on Him.

Now, I know that some people find that picture imagining in the way I have just described is not helpful for them. It is, after all, only a tool. Here are a few other 'tools' which you might find useful to bring you to that same point Z.

The Jesus Prayer

This is a prayer from Christian East Europe which those of you who prefer praying in a deeper, inner silence

might like to use. However, one thing is common with
the meditation – you must still your body and mind
using the relaxation skills I have described earlier in this
chapter.

When I use the Jesus prayer and when my body has
become still, I find it helpful to focus my mind on a single
object, either in my mind's eye, or by looking directly at
something. In that latter case, I should look at a cross, a
lighted candle or perhaps a flower. I look at my object
until my mind is quite still. It is then time to 'feed our
mind', but instead of filling it with a meditation picture,
we concentrate rather on our breathing in this sort of
way. First of all, breathe deeply but naturally from your
diaphragm so that the air is filling all of your lungs; pause
for three or four seconds between breathing in and
breathing out. Get used to the rhythm. Practise it. It is no
more than a skill and will in itself make you feel more
peaceful than you did before.

The next stage is to link a simple prayer with your
breathing. So, when you breathe in, you pray in your
mind, 'Lord Jesus Christ, Son of the living God', PAUSE,
and when you breathe out, pray, 'Have mercy on me, a
sinner'. (You can, of course, shorten these phrases if your
breathing time is short.)

Stay there, still before the Lord, repeating that prayer.
It is a tool to bring you to a humble expectation that
the Lord will work within you, but it is done without
'mental pictures'.

In the first place, when we breathe in, we *confess* who
Jesus is. He is Lord, Christ, Son of the living God. Right
use of the prayer will therefore include a true ac-
knowledgment of who He is. Then as we breathe out, we
confess who we are, sinners, and thereby owning
ourselves we place ourselves in our rightful relationship
to the Lord.

If we use the 'Jesus prayer' without that sense of
relationship between the Lord and ourselves, it would
merely be a babble, a meaningless mantra. When we use

it properly, it then becomes a means of moving our hearts and minds into their true place before the Lord Jesus. We shall know with mind, heart and soul, our whole being, that He is Lord and Saviour, and that we are the humble sinners whom He loves.

Yet once that knowing has happened, we have linked ourselves to how Jesus demonstrated His relationship to His Father when He came for baptism, for although He was without sin, He came and lovingly and humbly declared Himself to be subject to His heavenly Father.

But there is a little more in the prayer which can help those who do not find meditation useful, and that is the phrase, 'Have mercy on me'. Of course, that means asking for forgiveness, but for the Greek Christians who discovered this way of praying, mercy and grace are almost identical words, and grace is another way of asking for the Holy Spirit to come into our lives. So when this prayer is used, not only are we establishing in humility our relationship with our Lord, but we are also pleading for the Holy Spirit to come, cleanse and revive us.

Notice again the parallel with Jesus's baptism. He stood there waiting for and expecting the Holy Spirit to come upon Him, so we, too, can use the 'Jesus prayer' to bring us to that same goal, that point Z, where we wait humbly and expectantly on the Lord. The 'Jesus prayer', then, is a quiet way, which without the use of our imagination, brings and keeps us where we may well receive a baptism experience.

Praise and Worship

Since praise and worship are associated with singing, movement, dancing, clapping and so on, this seems to be taking a totally different direction from meditation and the Jesus prayer. Naturally, we offer praise to the Lord for no other reason than that He is the Lord. After all, worship comes from combining 'worth' with 'ship', which means giving someone their due. Nevertheless, the heart and reality of praise and worship is not the form or the way it is offered to God, but rather the relationship between the worshipper and the Lord God. Any style of worship, whether it is a wonderful rendering of a religious masterpiece by a great cathedral choir, or the informal jubilee of guitars and charismatic choruses, if it is not offered to God by folk who know who He is and who they are in relation to Him, is empty, null and void. The test of the reality of worship must never be how *we* feel when for example we have heard Handel's 'Messiah'. Handel did not write that great work to entertain an audience, nor should we respond to it as if it were composed for our 'uplift'. True worship will bring us first of all into a fresh personal realisation of the lordship of Jesus Christ and the majesty of our heavenly Father. Worship opens the window of heaven to give us a glimpse of God. When that happens, and I know that it does not happen every time, but when it does, our praise and worship will flow from our heartfelt knowledge that Jesus is Lord and our adoration will be in gratitude to Him, that as unworthy as we are, He has made us sons of God. The 'feel' of such worship is that we know the greatness of our God, and in knowing precisely that, see ourselves as we really are. When Isaiah caught a vision of God in the temple, he, too, saw God's majesty, but at the same time realised how unworthy he was.

The Book of Revelation is full of examples of praise and worship, acknowledging who God is and the lowliness of our status in His presence.

And the twenty-four elders who sit on their thrones before God *fell on their faces* and worshipped God, saying, 'We give thanks to thee, Lord God Almighty, who art and who wast, that thou hast taken thy great power and begun to reign' (Rev. 11:16–17; my italics).

And all the angels stood round the throne and round the elders and the four living creatures, and *they fell on their faces* before the throne and worshipped God, saying, 'Amen! Blessing and glory and wisdom and thanksgiving and honour and power and might be to our God for ever and ever! Amen' (Rev. 7:11–12; my italics).

Falling on their faces was an expression of their worship of God. But what does it express? Their knowledge of the greatness of the Lord, yes, but *also their sense of unworthiness to look upon His face*. Their worship proclaims the majesty of God and their own humility.

Yet the worshipper's experience of the greatness of God and his own humility is precisely the experience common to both meditation and the Jesus prayer – for they, too, take us to a humble waiting on Him who is Lord. How many of you have, like me, been worshipping and praising God sometimes even very loudly and noisily when quite suddenly, a deep waiting silence has fallen on all those present? At times like that, we are all profoundly aware of God's presence. It is the time when some may fall on their knees, others may prostrate themselves. It is the time when we know if anyone prays out loud or starts singing, it would be totally out of place. I want you to catch in your memory that moment when you were deeply silent and waiting because you knew the Lord was present. That is point Z. Praise has taken us to the edge of our faith-levels, there to wait on God to meet us with the Holy Spirit. And as we wait, conscious of who He is, and when there is an expectation that the Spirit will come, we may well witness 'baptism experiences'. It is in moments of worship like this that we do see healings and miracles. There could be revelation, new insights and new knowledge granted. People may weep, they may be filled with joy. Perhaps all this is rarer than it should be, yet praise and worship should bring us at least occasionally to such meeting-points with God. May God forgive us for ever being satisfied with 'services' which will never bring us to the living Lord because we shall not move into risky areas to explore the majesty of God.

Some years ago, I read an amusing but devastating story. A Christian from overseas visited a typically English church. At the door after the service, the vicar asked him what he thought about the morning's worship.

The visitor replied, 'Your God is too small.'

I appreciate that some of you may be in no position to influence the worship offered in your church, but we *can* do a lot about our own personal praise. However, I am sure that even if you have experienced too many tired, dull and uninspiring services, there has been perhaps one occasion when through the worship you caught a glimpse of God. Try and recall how you felt when you did. Catch the moment. Do you remember a humble waiting on the Lord just before He met you in the way special to you that He did? That is point Z.

Now the good news is that although we should experience those times in congregational praise, we are not limited to that. We can meet Him in that way in our personal worship and devotion.

May I suggest you do something quite simple in your private devotions? Find a place where you are confident that you are alone with the Lord and where you will not be interrupted. Then, when you pray, speak your words *out loud*. When you worship or praise, *sing out* your hymn or chorus. Initially you might feel somewhat foolish, but I have found that when I worship like that it helps *my whole self* to become focused on the Lord. In other words, praising in that way helps me to realise who God is and who I am in relationship to Him.

Try it and see, and when you have tried it many times, let yourself become aware of those moments of inner stillness and quiet as you know you are waiting on the Lord. That is point Z.

Of course, being at point Z, whether via meditation,

the Jesus prayer, or praise, does not and can never guarantee that we shall meet the Holy Spirit, but it is the station where we catch the train.

10

KEEPING IN MIND

The previous chapter has, I hope, helped you prepare to meet the Holy Spirit. We can only come humbly and expectant on God, simply asking Him for His Spirit. Baptism experiences are totally under God's control, so even if we believe we are somewhat accomplished at waiting on the Lord, there is no guarantee that we shall meet Him. Indeed, there may be long periods of time when we shall never experience God at all. As I have said previously, that may well mean no more than that we simply need time to consolidate what the Spirit has already given us.

This chapter is about consolidating what we have received already. Whatever faith-level we are on, every one of us needs to let the Holy Spirit work those new insights and fresh knowledge into us in such a way that they become part and parcel of our way of perceiving and understanding the world.

God does not grant us baptism experiences for their own sake. We do not embrace a religion of unrelated, individualistic feelings. Rather, baptism experiences are shots of God's power which will work change through our senses and in our minds, leading us into putting on the mind of Christ. We need time to consolidate what the Holy Spirit is doing.

This chapter is also concerned with refreshing or re-stating what we once received from the Lord, but thought we had lost.

We all know that progress up the steps of faith is rather

more complicated than simply putting one foot forward after the other. So often we feel we might well have gone forward one step, but have then found ourselves bumping down a couple. We slip back. Old ways have a nasty habit of tripping us. We find ourselves thinking like we used to do.

Of course, some of the reasons why we slip back relate to our deeper need to confess and to renounce old ways, but one thing is certain. Even though we may rightly believe we have gone far from what the Lord once showed us and did for us, *He will never withdraw what He did in our lives.* 'For the gifts and the call of God are irrevocable' (Rom. 11:29).

The spiritual discipline which helps bring about consolidation of what the Spirit has given us, and helps to refresh and restate what we once received is what is called 'remembrance'.

'Remembrance'

The farthest thing from my mind is everything we in England associate with 'Remembrance Sunday'. I am sure the services around November to remember the war dead are very important and moving. I am sure it is a good thing to remember past victories over evil and to recall those who gave their lives. But the Biblical understanding of 'remembrance' has a far richer and extensive meaning than what is encapsulated in that particular Sunday near Armistice Day.

One of my delights in visiting the elderly is to take notice of the photographs of all their family. On the mantelpiece, china cupboard and piano there is usually a whole row full of several generations of wedding pictures, and scores of those seemingly mass-produced photographs of junior school-children.

'Who,' I ask, 'is that delightful person over there?'

'Well,' beams back the delighted lady, 'that's my

granddaughter. And she is doing ever so well. Do you know she qualified as a nurse last year?'

'Well, I never,' say I.

'And do you know,' she now continues, 'she met such a lovely man that they got married last April. Would you like to see the wedding photographs?'

'Of course,' I say, but think, 'what have I let myself in for now?'

And out comes the wedding album. Ceremoniously, I am beckoned to sit by her side, as she pours out the details and circumstances of each picture, pointing out to me people whom I have never seen and am unlikely ever to see. Naturally, I am polite and courteous. After all, that's what vicars are supposed to be. I am sure you can appreciate that for her all of those memories have come back afresh into her mind. She can remember and feel her joy on seeing how beautiful her granddaughter looked. She can remember, though she will not tell you, the little tear she shed as she was made aware of her marriage to her late husband 54 years ago this weekend. Those photographs cause her own memories to be stirred in her conscious mind. Those events in her past become richly present for her now. This is true of all of us and our photographs. We spend time in those cold dreary nights looking and laughing at our summer holiday pictures. They are our memories, but recalling them is the way of stirring up in us what the events meant for us at the time. Other people's photographs, however expertly taken, are never as interesting as ours, out of focus and be-headed as they may be. After all, they are records of *our* memories.

It is that sense of remembering I want us to explore as being God's means of keeping our minds fresh in Him. I mean 'remembering' as recalling what God has done for us in our past. *Such remembering will release afresh the experience of those events to give us a living expectation in God.*

There is not a lot of information about Mary, the Mother of Jesus, in the Bible, but there are some helpful hints about her style of spirituality in the first two chapters of Luke's Gospel. Particularly there are these verses:

> Luke 1:28–9: And he came to her and said, 'Hail, O favoured one, the Lord is with you.' But she was greatly troubled at the saying and *considered in her mind* what sort of greeting this might be (my italics).

> Luke 2:19: [After the shepherds had visited the infant Jesus] But Mary *kept all these things, pondering them* in her heart (my italics).

> Luke 2:51: [After the boy Jesus was lost in the Temple] He went down with them and came to Nazareth, and was obedient to them; and his mother *kept all these things in her heart* (my italics).

Mary had no photographs, but she had abundantly rich memories of what the Lord God had done for her in her life. Those great acts of God in her were not events which she simply let go over her head, or even worse took for granted. She, as it says, kept all those things. They were her photograph album, imprinted in her heart. What joy she would have experienced, what feelings would be released, what fresh gratitude she would feel to God as she remembered! The verse says, 'Mary kept all these things, *pondering* them in her heart'. How much she must have remembered in the quiet of her own room of what God had done for her. What did she feel when she heard the familiar stories in the synagogue of the barren Sarah giving birth to Isaac, of infertile Hannah producing Samuel the servant of the Lord? What did she feel when she heard the reading of the prophet Isaiah: 'The Lord himself will give you a sign. Behold, a young woman shall conceive and bear a son, and shall call his name Immanuel' (Isa. 7:14)?

Can't you feel her excitement, her emotions? Do you see how Mary remembers what the Lord has done

for her, and how that recalled memory creates fresh
excitement and joy in her God?

I can see her joy spilling out all over her kinswoman
Elizabeth!

> She [Elizabeth] exclaimed with a loud cry 'Blessed are
> you among women . . . And blessed is she who be-
> lieved that there would be a fulfilment of what was
> spoken to her from the Lord'.
> And Mary said, 'My soul magnifies the Lord, and my
> spirit rejoices in God my Saviour . . .' (Luke 1:42–7).

Mary, I believe, rejoiced in God because she *kept and
pondered all these things*. That is the clue to her spiritual
vitality! And it is the key to ours. Mary knew how to keep
fresh her knowledge and love for God *by remembering
what He had done for her*. I can see her in her old age with
someone like Luke at her side asking her about her
'photographs', and all those memories and feelings
simply being released.

Such remembering is not merely nostalgia. It isn't a
looking with tears in our eyes and a lump in our throat at
something wonderful which happened many years ago
and has no effect on us now. A true sense of remembering makes what God did in us in the past, *present yet
again*. When we remember, the Holy Spirit re-creates that
same sense of joy and wonder in God we first experienced. Perhaps we can let the Lord's work in us slip too
easily into the distant past, and leaving it there, let it have
no effect in our lives. I suppose our minds are like busy
streets, no matter how clean and fresh they once were,
the ideas and philosophies of our world will soon pollute
them. However, when we remember who God is and
what He has done in our lives, pondering like Mary did,
then the Holy Spirit cleanses our streets, enabling them
again to think in God-centred ways. If you are like me,
the streets of your mind will need cleaning very regularly. But it's not just a matter of cleansing. When the

Holy Spirit moves and works, He creates. He created order out of chaos at the beginning of the creation, and as we 'remember', He will create new minds in us. Consider Mary again. Thirty-three years after her pregnancy, she was there at the cross. She was there, too, in the upper room with the disciples waiting for the Holy Spirit to come. The fruit of many years of remembering and pondering?

Remembering with Scripture

We know little about Mary except that she would have been a devout Jew, brought up in the traditions of that faith, attending synagogue, making pilgrimage to Jerusalem, and keeping the festivals. Have you ever wondered why God asked His people actually to perform and keep those traditions and ceremonies? Naturally, He wants us to praise and worship Him for who He is, but since worship places us in right relationship with Him, we, too, shall receive something from Him by doing those things. God uses the things we offer to Him to stir up our memories of what He has done for us. God can use our worship to renew our minds by helping us remember.

We can especially recognise this when the Bible is read and expounded, and certainly the services Mary attended at synagogue would have included reading from the Old Testament. Of course, we read the Scriptures to instruct us in all godliness, but one of the main purposes of the public (and indeed private) reading of the Bible is to let it remind us of what the Lord has done for us in the past and so rekindle our faith and hope in Him. Mary's faith must have been renewed in the face of the gossip and accusations of immorality when she heard the reading from the prophet Isaiah foretelling that a young girl would conceive and bear a son. The spoken word from Scripture would have refreshed and renewed the word spoken to her by the archangel Gabriel. God gave us Scripture to create faith in Him, but also to renew our faith in Him for what He has done. The Bible is God's spoon to stir up our memories so we shall 'remember'.

Mary would have responded to hearing the Scriptures in two ways. First of all, she was a daughter of Israel, a member of God's chosen people, so she would have rejoiced over what He had done in her nation's past. However, she also had *personal* experience of what the Lord could do – He had acted mightily in her – so she would have a personal response to Scriptures which resonated with her own knowledge of God. This is like listening to a group of people sharing experiences of their summer holidays. We identify with that group discussion because we, too, went on holiday, but then someone says, 'Last year we went to Sweden' and our interest suddenly quickens because that was where we went, too. Mary would have identified with those Scriptures telling what God had done for her people because it was her race, but her heart would quicken when she heard the stories which reminded her of what God had done for her. 'For he who is mighty has done great things *for me*' (Luke 1:49; my italics).

Sabbath after Sabbath, the Jewish people would hear the Scriptures telling them what God had done for them so they could rejoice in that they were members of that saved nation as they remembered together, *but the Christian has an extra dimension to his or her rejoicing in God*. That extra is the Mary-dimension, for although like the Jews, we Christians remember and rejoice in God for what Christ has done for His people, the Church, nevertheless, *we also remember and rejoice over what He has done for each one of us as individual persons*. For we must always remember that Christians are not like the Jews who automatically become members of the Old Testament people of God by simply being born into a Jewish family; Christians become members of the New Testament people of God by individually and separately coming to personal faith in Jesus Christ as Lord and Saviour. Each one of us has a story, dramatic or not, of how we came to believe in Christ. We all have some sort of baptism experience. Consequently when Scriptures are read, and the saving work of Jesus Christ is expounded from the pulpit, not only will they be means of remembering what the Lord has done for the Church and world, but times of remembering and therefore recalling what He has done in and for each one of us. We need to hear the good news of salvation proclaimed, not only to give opportunity to those who have never heard it to respond, but to let it stir up the memory of our own salvation and so rekindle and remind us of who the Lord is and what He can do.

> Therefore I intend always to remind you of these things, though you know them and are established in the truth that you have. I think it right, as long as I am in this body, to *arouse you by way of reminder* . . . And I will see to it that after my departure you may be able at any time to *recall these* things (2 Pet. 1:12–15; my italics).

But as far as we, who have already experienced something of God are concerned, the Spirit through the Scriptures will only recall what we 'ponder in our hearts'.

Most ministers have to spend a fair deal of time with depressed church members, whose moods vary according to the barometer. I do not wish to appear to be unkind or simplistic, but it seems to me that one common factor in such people is that in being preoccupied with their present problems, they easily *forget* what God did for them even in their recent past. Of course, I realise that such people may find it difficult to believe and accept our heavenly Father does care for them, but if an inability to ponder on what He has done results in so much deadness, how much more renewed life and outlook will be created when we do ponder on the great acts of God for us?

The Bible and the preached Word of God act as stimuli, releasing the emotions, feelings and mind-attitudes we experienced when we met the Lord. Our minds and outlooks are refreshed and reordered in what they know of God and of His ways. Jesus Christ promised His disciples that He would send His Holy Spirit to 'bring to your remembrance all that I have said to you'.

At the time of writing, a Korean minister is a guest in my church. He has come to learn English, and he is finding it quite difficult. For some weeks, he makes considerable progress, and speaks English quite fluently, but then, a Korean family will invite him out for an evening and, quite naturally, he speaks Korean all the time. The effect on his English is devastating! His Korean thought and speech forms take control again and oust the English he has learnt.

This applies to how we Christians think and understand the world. We have all been born again into the Kingdom of God, but the world around quickly tries to teach us its way of thinking. However, if we have regular meetings with those who speak *our* true language our 'foreign' tongue, too, will be ousted.

If then we desire to keep our minds 'renewed', we must hear God's Scriptures being read and expounded in such a way that it stirs up our faith. That means we must be with God's people Sunday by Sunday where that happens. We must make sure private or small-group Bible-study is part of our regular spiritual diet – not out of a sense of duty, but because looking at God's Word 'reminds' us of what He has done for us.

Remembering with Holy Communion/the Lord's Supper

The Jewish traditions celebrated what God had done in their nation's past, and even today, the Jews celebrate the Passover which reminds them how God saved their people from slavery in Egypt. Yet, the Passover ceremony is fundamentally the occasion when the Jewish family *makes remembrance* of what God did for their nation. I am sure that Mary would have made such remembrance with her Son, Jesus. But the feel of the passover celebration is not one of distance and separation from what happened to their ancestors thousands of years ago, but rather one of racial solidarity with them. What happened to their ancestors also happened to them, so Passover is a celebration of God's rescue of all the Jewish people, and not only those who were actually in Egypt. This remembering the Passover makes that 'past' saving work present for them. Thus, present-day Jews celebrate *their* rescue from slavery, sharing in their nation's joy from the past and so refreshing their faith that He who saved them once, can and will act to save them now and in the future.

As you and I draw on personal memories, the Jews draw on a *corporate* memory – a memory which belongs not to individuals but to the whole people as a unity, and which today's Jewish race may now recall and celebrate. It is their salvation event. So one of the greatest sins Israel, the people of God, could do was to *forget* what He had done. Certainly the Old Testament declares over and over again that the people of Israel offended God because they did not remember what He had done. They forgot what He had done for Abraham, Isaac and Jacob. They forgot that it was He, the Lord, who had rescued them from slavery.

Did they forget in the sense that they had no memory or knowledge about what had happened, or did they forget by simply not bothering to recall His saving events so they were not re-created in the people's mind? However it happened, one thing is certain, forgetting is the pathway to spiritual disaster. If the streets of our mind are not cleansed by remembrance, then sooner or later the pollutions of the world around will corrupt our minds. The people of Israel left the Lord and turned to the worship and service of Baal; we for our part will take on God-less ways of understanding our world. So no wonder God's call is: 'Remember the days of old, consider the years of many generations; ask your father and he will show you; your elders and they will tell you' (Deut. 32:7).

The Lord God gave the Jews the Passover meal so they would have opportunity to remember and realise afresh what He had done for them. The same Lord has given a remembrance meal to the New Testament people of God. We call it the Lord's Supper, Holy Communion, the Eucharist, the breaking of bread. Whatever name you give it, it is an act of remembrance given by God as an opportunity for Christians to be refreshed and reminded of what Jesus did for us all on Calvary.

The Lord Jesus gave us our 'remembrance meal' towards the end of a Passover meal. The upper room in Jerusalem had been prepared for Jesus and his disciples to celebrate the Passover. They had already given thanks and remembered how God had rescued their people from slavery. The unleavened bread had been broken, the bitter herbs eaten, the sop 'for the favourite one' given; the remembrance was being enacted.

Perhaps they talked together and shared the story of what God had done for their nation. Perhaps they still wondered when Elijah or the Messiah would come . . .

But then in the midst of all that 'remembering', 'The Lord Jesus on the night when He was betrayed, took bread, and when he had given thanks, he broke it and said, "This is my body which is for you. Do this in remembrance of me" . . . For as often as you eat this bread and drink the cup, you proclaim the Lord's death until he comes' (1 Cor. 11:24–6).

We are in the middle of *remembrance* – moving from the great deliverance of the Passover to Calvary. Jesus gave us His Supper so that we should remember what He did once and for all on the cross, and by remembering the cross be refreshed and reminded of His love for us.

There is, of course, a major difference between Christians and Jews – the Jews identify with the Passover through their racial unity – but we Christians identify with the cross by coming to a *personal* realisation of forgiveness and liberation. The Lord's Supper is only for those who believe in Christ, who accept that Jesus won forgiveness and brought redemption for all who 'call on His name'. Consequently, when Christians remember what the Lord Jesus did on the cross, they may identify with it in the way the Jews link with the Passover, but they will also recall how and when they first experienced the Lord's forgiveness for themselves. So besides being a time for remembering how God saved His 'people', it is also a time to remember how He saved *persons*, you and me. We are recalling the story of our own salvation.

What a tragedy, what a mockery when a Holy Communion service becomes a mere recitation or an empty ritual. What a sham if there is no exhortation or even opportunity for those present to let the Holy Spirit bring fresh to our minds that great and glorious work of God when Jesus died and rose for us. But what a loss, too, if the Lord's Supper becomes a dull, sombre occasion, perhaps rightly reminding us of our sin, but not giving space for those refreshing and renewing bursts of joy and thanksgiving which will happen when we let the Holy Spirit renew in our minds what Jesus did for us. After all, Holy Communion is celebrated on Sundays to remind us of new life and new creation, and not on Friday, no matter how great the necessity of the cross. The Lord Jesus gave us His Supper so that we should remember, and, in remembering, experience the renewing work of God's Spirit in our minds. We become mind-full of what He can do! Holy Communion is our enacted photograph, reminding us of what the Lord Jesus did for us on the cross.

There are two dimensions then when we come together for the Lord's Supper. First of all, we remember the great deliverance which Christ has worked for His

Church and for all mankind. His blood was shed for many for the forgiveness of sins. Second, we come thanking God for what He has done for us as individuals, remembering how we came to know forgiveness from Jesus for ourselves. The loaf is blessed, but broken for all to share. We draw near with faith, remembering that though He gave His body for the life of the world, we shall receive a morsel, a fragment of that loaf, knowing from our hearts that He gave His life for us.

So we do not 'neglecting to meet together, as is the habit of some' (Heb. 10:25) because remembering what the Lord has done will indeed 'stir up one another to love and good works' (v. 24).

Of course, I readily admit that we do not experience such refreshing and renewing every time we remember what the Lord has done for us, but if we never take time to remember then we shall forget what He has done and our minds will take up the prevailing attitudes of the world around.

So then, I encourage you to keep your minds renewed 'to present your bodies as a living sacrifice, holy and acceptable to God, which is your spiritual worship' (Rom. 12:1). Make sure that Sunday after Sunday you join God's people who are making remembrance of what the Lord Jesus has done. They will be making remembrance through preaching and the sacrament of bread and wine, but cling to those who celebrate with joy, thanksgiving and expectation.

Yet, of course, there is a proper place for our own remembering of what the Lord has done in us individually. Mary kept all these things in her heart and pondered on them, and so, too, must we if we want to preserve our spiritual freshness and alertness to the moving of His Spirit. Everyone of us has his or her story to tell of God's dealings in our lives. It might be a dramatic conversion story; it might be a slow dawning of the truth of the Lord Jesus; it might be how we saw the Lord Jesus in the life of a Christian; it might be how we received a great flood of comfort in our time of need. It might be one of many events, but it is the event or events of the story of the Lord God dealing with *your* life. Only you can re-experience your memories. Remember the old lady who showed me her photograph album? My interest and enthusiasm could never match hers because they were her memories, not mine. If I turned up with my photograph album, we could have a lovely time together, thinking about old times.

We cannot live off other people's experiences. They can, of course, encourage us to see that God is far bigger than we ever thought, but in the end it is only as you sit down, kneel or whatever and recall what God did for *you*, what He promised *you*, that He can rekindle in your heart and mind who and what He is for you. Remembrance keeps you afresh in His purposes for you and your world.

11

KNOWING IN PART

For now we see in a mirror dimly, but then face to face.
Now I know in part, then I shall understand fully
(1 Cor. 13:12).

This chapter is about how our renewed/renewing minds
perceive and understand the world. However, before we
start, I want to emphasise, along with St Paul, the partial
nature of our perception. Our present understanding, no
matter which faith-level we are on, is never perfect or
totally true, because perfection will only come when we
see God face to face. So any mind under renewal will of
necessity be a mixture of light and darkness. Like a
candle shining in a dark room, the renewing light we
receive shows up shapes and objects we never realised
were there. Nevertheless, we shall not see the detail of
those shapes and objects until daylight has come. So
what I am writing is based on how I personally see things
at this present time. I do not claim to be absolutely right. I
can only write about insights and new outlooks which are
relative to my own experience of God. If I had written this
chapter some years ago, it might well have been quite
different, and no doubt those of you who have more
experience of the Lord may well see in all charity that I
have much more to learn. However, please bear with me
as I reflect on some insights, which can of course only be a
'knowing in part'.

Let us look at the faith-growth diagram again.

```
                                          Faith-level C
                                              |
                      Faith-level B            ↓
                          |
    Faith-level A          ↓
        |
         ↓
```

A person who is at faith-level C has undergone two baptism experiences taking him from A to B and then from B to C. He has his own evidence of meeting the Holy Spirit, and has asked the Spirit to renew his mind through baptism experiences.

If that is the case, those two baptism experiences will include putting on something *more* of the mind of Christ. The *extra* he received was not a gradual change, but as the diagram shows, a sudden input of more of the Lord's mind. He should, therefore, have a definite change in his understanding of the world. If then we can discover through our own baptism experiences what new perceptions we have, what new ways we have in responding to life, we may well have an indication of what it is to see and understand the world through the Lord's eyes. If you like, those sudden inputs are 'bits' from the Lord's mind. Study the 'bits' and you will have a good understanding of His mind.

What I want to share with you are my own reflections on my own experiences. I ask you to reflect on yours and discover those things for yourself. When we are discovering how our minds have been changed, we are not concerned with mere ideas, but of thinking and behaving in our world. Our minds do not become narrower by exclusion, but richer by integration.

Integration

As the Holy Spirit takes us up to higher faith and knowledge levels, we shall discover at least two things when we look back at where we were. In the diagram, when you are at level C, look back at yourself on levels A and B. First of all, you will wonder and marvel at why you never saw what you now realise is obvious.

Second, and far more importantly, your new understanding of God and His world will include a thorough reassessment of what you thought at lower levels of faith. This assessment will usually result in one of two courses of action. You will either *reject* previous experiences or *integrate* them into how you now think. For example, when someone has a conversion experience, they may well wonder why they had never been told before about Jesus Christ even though they had been attending church for years. Of course, the Gospel message may well have been proclaimed regularly, but for some reason they never 'heard' it. So how might they respond now they have been converted?

First, they might look back on their previous church-going faith-level and assess it. If they do that with distaste and anger, they will probably reject their local church for failing to bring them to conversion, particularly if they were brought to faith in a different situation. They will probably leave their local church and join another. That is the way of rejection.

The wiser convert, however, might look at his 'church-going' more constructively and discover what could have been helpful in bringing about what he now knows. He will want to know if there was anything at all useful and formative in those years of merely attending church. He will turn over in his mind everything that has happened over the years, and he might recognise that even then the Lord was preparing him to meet Himself.

So what is happening? The convert is looking for parts of his past which he can *integrate* into his present thinking.

'Yes,' he decides, 'that was unhelpful, but that was good.'

Indeed, though many Christians may well be able to

name a time and place where and when they met the Lord, they can often identify formative and important events as necessary preparations to meeting the Lord. However, such identification usually *comes after* their conversion experience. Before they met the Lord, those events might not have been so important, but with a new outlook they take on a different meaning. They begin to see that perhaps it was the Lord who led them to that church; perhaps it was He who introduced them to that particular person. It is not unusual for people to believe that in one way or another the Lord was with them well before they ever confessed His name.

So what are they doing? They are integrating their past experiences into their new understanding and perceptions.

Of course that does not mean that everything they thought or did before was good or true – there will be much that has to be left behind – nevertheless, their renewed mind will discover what was good and incorporate it into its newer way of understanding. That is integration.

Embracing ambiguity

The battle of the mind for Western Christians is the issue of whether or not God is involved in His creation. It focuses quite specifically on miracles, signs and wonders. Does God do them? Now, I know many genuine born-again Christians who really doubt whether God will work signs and wonders today. (A doubt which is revealed by the challenge of the 'miracle-test'.) Such people, therefore, hold two sets of beliefs. First of all, they know personally the reality of conversion, so they have had at least one baptism experience. Second, they hold another insight, another way of ordering and perceiving life which excludes or denies the possibility of God's activity to heal. This insight might be theirs simply

because they have absorbed our prevailing secular culture which leaves no room for God; or they may have
theological reasons; or yet again, their own experience of
praying for the sick has never ended in any healings.
Whatever the reason, it will be a 'reason' – the mind will
have made such thinking self-consistent. Consequently,
our born-again Christian may well have doubts which are
quite genuine.

I have described in previous chapters how the Lord can
meet with someone and move them up to the next
faith-level. When that happens and they know God can
and will act miraculously, how will that sort of person
perceive how he used to think? In my experience he will
either reject his previous way of thinking, or integrate
what was true into his higher view of things. I am
suggesting integration is more of the mind of Christ than
total outright rejection.

How will he then see his former disbelief? Of course,
old insights which are misleading or false must be rejected, but before we do that, *we must examine them with
our higher faith to see if they embody any truth which might be
part of the way we now understand how God works in the world*.

Perhaps before our born-again Christian totally rejects
his former doubts, he should ponder just a while to
discover any hidden truth buried in them.

*Perhaps those doubts about miracles are concerned with an
anxiety that there is indeed an ambiguity about the healing
ministry*. The facts of ministry declare that not everyone
who receives prayer is healed or even improves in health,
while others are definitely restored to health. This ambiguity has to be faced squarely. Why are some healed
and others not? Of course, since most of us prefer things
to be black or white and dislike ambiguity of any kind, it
becomes a great temptation to blame people or situations
when healing does not happen. My heart aches for the
sick and suffering when the visiting healer proclaims, 'If
you have the faith, the Lord will always heal.' So what
happens when 'nothing' happens?

In my ministry, I have seen the faithless healed miraculously and the faithful die miserably. I do not know why some are healed and others are not. That is the ambiguity our born-again Christian must embrace into his new faith in the healing Lord. He must see that though he *knows* the Lord can and will heal, there will be some who are not healed.

Integration in the New Testament

The New Testament knows this sort of integration which looks back searching for truth and embraces ambiguity. Take, for example, the problem whether or not Christians should obey the Law of Moses.

In the Old Testament, man's faith in God was expressed by pleasing Him through keeping all its rules and regulations. There can be no doubt that the New Testament believes those Laws were given by God to Moses. So what happened when Law-abiding Jews were raised to a higher level of faith in Jesus Christ? How did they react towards their previous faith-level when they looked back and saw how they used to try and please God?

The New Testament knows both rejection and integration.

There were those who totally *rejected the Law* and its demands. By the end of the first century, some churches had moved towards total lawlessness and immorality since they held they were no longer bound by religious restrictions. That is the problem the Book of Revelation tackles in its first few chapters.

So John hears the Lord declaring to the church at Pergamum,

> But I have a few things against you: you have some there who hold the teaching of Balaam, who taught Balak to put a stumbling block before the sons of Israel, that they might eat food sacrificed to idols and practise immorality (Rev. 2:14).

And to the church in Thyatira,

> But I have this against you, that you tolerate the
> woman Jezebel, who calls herself a prophetess and is
> teaching and beguiling my servants to practise im-
> morality and to eat food sacrificed to idols (Rev. 2:20).

Those churches had rejected the Law of Moses.

Even in His ministry, the Lord Jesus had said, 'Think
not that I have come to abolish the law and the prophets; I
have not come to abolish them but to fulfil them' (Matt.
5:17).

Jewish believers may not abandon the Law! So how
could they integrate it into their Christian faith?

Let us take St Paul as an example and discover how he
embraced the Law and the ambiguities Moses' teachings
produce.

Paul, an orthodox, Law-abiding Jew, met the risen
Lord on the Damascus road, and, as we all know, was
catapulted up to a higher faith-level. It was his 'baptism
experience'. Consequently, his new-found faith was no
longer based on pleasing God by keeping rules and
regulations, but on experiencing the Lord's love and
mercy and living them for others. So what did St Paul
think about his previous Jewish ways?

The first thing is clear. He viewed them through his
new understanding, a new outlook formed by an encounter with the Holy Spirit who had 'shed love abroad
into his heart'. In the following statements we see that is
exactly how he understood the Law.

> Galatians 5:14: For the whole law is fulfilled in one
> word, 'You shall love your neighbour as yourself.'
> Romans 13:10: Love does no wrong to a neighbour,
> therefore love is the fulfilling of the law.

Paul knew that the influx of God's love he had received
completed what he was hopelessly striving for as an

orthodox Jew. It would have been unthinkable for him to go back to how he used to live, so no wonder he became angry with those who tried to bring his churches 'under Law'. Paul knew his conversion was no mere *addition* to what he had as a Jew, but a tremendous spiritual breakthrough to a new level of faith which made what he was before a pale shadow.

However, Paul never rejected the Law. He looked back on his old faith and *integrated* it into his new outlook of love for Christ.

First of all, he looked for what was good within the Law.

This is the sort of conclusion he came to:

Now before faith came, we were confined under the Law, kept under restraint until faith should be revealed. So that the Law was our *custodian* until Christ came, that we might be justified by faith (Gal. 3:23–4; my italics).

Thus, Paul recognised the positive contribution of the Law of Moses in his own spiritual development. It was a necessary preliminary stage before he came to faith in Christ, but it was only a stage, a stepping-stone. The Law looked after him as a guardian cares for a child until it comes to maturity.

Paul honoured his Jewish traditions by integrating them into the way of faith.

Second, integration can mean accepting ambiguity. So what truth from the Law needs to be embraced within our certainty of God's love? Is there a hidden truth in the Law which we must accept?

In Romans 7:12, Paul wrote, 'So the Law is holy, and the commandment is holy and just and good.' That is straightforward. God gave us His commandments so we would know how to obey Him. But that is *not* the hidden truth. That's the *plain* truth. Paul knows what the *concealed* truth is.

He also wrote in Romans 7:7–10 (my italics):

Yet, *if it had not been for the law, I should not have known sin.* I should not have known what it is to covet if the law had not said 'You shall not covet.' But sin, *finding opportunity in the commandment,* wrought in me all kinds of covetousness. Apart from the law sin lies dead. I was once alive apart from the law, but *when the commandment came, sin revived and I died*; the very commandment which promised life proved to be death to me.

What is the hidden truth in the Law?

Just this: *The Law reveals and demonstrates our sinfulness.* I suspect *that* is the truth the Law rejectors wanted to avoid, but that is precisely the truth we must embrace when we integrate the Law into a higher faith-level of knowing God's love in Christ.

If the Jewish traditions, if the Ten Commandments, are the climax of man's ability to draw close to God, then *this hidden truth declares we are all lost.* We are indeed wretched. 'Wretched man that I am!' wrote St Paul. 'Who will deliver me from this body of death?' (Rom. 7:24).

Why wretched? Because the Law teaches that God will not accept sinners into His presence.

So then, as far as the Law is concerned, it declares to us a fundamental doubt whether God would ever form a permanent relationship with us because of our sinfulness.

How then did St Paul embrace that uncertainty within his knowledge of Christ's love? *First* of all and above all, *he knew God had accepted him.* 'Yet,' Paul seems to declare, 'the Lord Jesus met me – despite all my sinfulness, despite my blindness to God's purposes, despite the fact that I was in hot pursuit of the first believers. Christ embraced me in His love.'

Wretched and miserable as he was, the Lord met him, brought him to our heavenly Father, forgave him his sins and filled him with His Holy Spirit. Paul experienced God's love for himself, and *he realised that such a love for him could more than cope with the ambiguity that he was indeed a sinner*.

But that is far from all that happens to our sinfulness. You will know for yourself when what happened to Paul in some way happens to you. You are overwhelmed with gratitude and joy for what the Lord has done for you, *because you know you are totally unworthy to have received any of it at all*. We know we are sinners. We know we are not perfect and never will be, yet God has declared us forgiven and cleansed by meeting us. The old Law condemned us for our sinfulness. It told us in no uncertain terms that God would never accept the sinful into His presence. But now, because of the Lord Jesus, that *total unworthiness revealed by the Law becomes the springboard for our wonder and joy in our God*, for though we should be justly and rightly rejected, nevertheless . . . nevertheless, God in His mercy and love has come to us and dwells in us by His Holy Spirit.

Our wretchedness shows us the greatness of God's love for us.

Back to Paul: 'But God shows His love for us in that while we were yet sinners, Christ died for us' (Rom. 5:8). And since we have been baptised into Him, 'There is therefore now no condemnation for those who are in Christ Jesus' (Rom. 8:1).

It is His amazing grace. The fact that we are so sinful shows us the wonder and the greatness of God's love for us. Our wretchedness before God is swept up into that higher knowledge that He loves us *so much* that He sent Jesus to die for us on the cross.

Christians are therefore a remarkable phenomenon. We are at the same time both sinners and united with God. But these two conditions do not have equal standing, because our sinfulness has been embraced by God's overwhelming and all-holding love for us. When God looks at us He no longer sees the sinner, but 'the sinner for whom Jesus died'. He looks on us 'as found in Him'.

And the marvel is that we know we *are* sinners! So no wonder our sense of unworthiness becomes the source of our joyful thanks to the Lord that He should die for one such as you or I. It was a great French philosopher who declared, 'Mankind is divided into two sorts of people. Sinners who think they are saints, and saints who know they are sinners.'

That is integration.

However, this book is not about equipping you with intellectual ideas about the mind or the Christian life. It is about renewing our outlook and therefore behaviour in this world. When Paul was embraced by the Lord's mercy and love on the Damascus road, his whole purpose and motivation for living were radically changed. His encounter with Christ, his baptism experience, opened his eyes to see in a different light. Not only would he think differently about the Christians he was persecuting, but he would see his past religious life with a new understanding, and a new course of action.

After this most orthodox of all Jews had met Christ, he knew that he was called to go to the non-Jewish nations, the Gentiles, and spread the good news of God's love for all mankind. A new mind generates new motivation and new action.

Paul realised that God's love in him would provide all the necessary energy and action to do everything the Ten Commandments said he must. A man who can write 1 Corinthians 13 knows from his heart that love completes everything the Law demands.

If then my insight is at least partially right, integration enriches our walk with God by incorporating old truth into the higher faith and knowledge the Lord has given us. I believe this way of sifting over our former beliefs, whatever those beliefs were, to see what has to be rejected, what has to be embraced, what hidden truth has to be accepted, is of the nature of the Lord's mind.

And He said to them, 'Therefore every scribe who has been trained for the kingdom of heaven is like a house-holder who brings out of his treasure what is *new* and what is *old*' (Matt. 13:52).

I am confident such integration is in accordance with the Lord's way of thinking. My confidence rests in what I see when I 'set my mind above where Christ is'.

Revelation 5:6 declares: 'I saw a Lamb standing, as though it had been slain'.

The ascended, glorified Jesus still bears the marks of the cross. He has not rejected His death, but embraced it into what He is now with our Father.

St John, too, informs us that the risen Lord still has pierced hands and side: 'He [Jesus] said to Thomas, "Put your finger here and see my hands; and put out your hand and place it in my side"' (20:27).

Not only His death, but the *manner* of His death has been integrated into the Resurrection. When the Holy Spirit came down into Jesus's tomb and raised Him up 'on high', He gave us the highest level of all to *understand the meaning of such a terrible tragic death*. The Resurrection interprets the Cross and gives it another meaning from the one it had before Easter Day. Without the Resurrection, Jesus's death was no more than one of the endless, innocent, painful executions many others have endured. It would have been totally futile. At the best, a good man dying for his beliefs.

Without the Resurrection, the cross is indeed the symbol of man's gross inhumanity to others. Without Easter, the cross is truly the sign of God's rejection of mankind.

'Cursed be every one who hangs on a tree' (Gal. 3:13).

The cross *is* a God-forsaken place.

That is why a crucified Christ is a 'stumbling block to the Jews'. How could someone whom the Law of God declares is cursed, be the one whom He sent? That is why an impotent Son of God, nailed to the gibbet, was 'folly to the Greeks'. How could a divine man be so weak as to accept suffering?

Without Resurrection, all that is true.

But with Resurrection, all the uncertainty and ambiguity is integrated into who the risen Lord is and given a new meaning:

> He carried our curse
>
> He is the expiation for our sins (1 John 2:2).
>
> The blood of Jesus his son cleanses us from all sin (1 John 1:7).
>
> For our sake he made him to be sin who knew no sin, so that in him we might become the righteousness of God (2 Cor. 5:21).

Resurrection declares that this was no innocent man being unjustly condemned to death on a cross, rather it was the Lamb of God, prepared before the foundation of the world, to take away our sins and offer forgiveness and reconciliation. '. . . this Jesus, delivered up *according to the definite plan and foreknowledge of God*' (Acts 2:23; my italics).

The cross, which was the symbol of our certain rejection by God, has been transformed by the Resurrection into the sign of our forgiveness and reconciliation.

So we set our eyes on the glorified Lord who bears the marks of the nails, but has given them a new meaning – a new meaning which offers forgiveness and reconciliation for all who put their trust in Him. He has baptised our sufferings and rejections and changed them into being mighty instruments to further God's purpose in this world.

That is integration.

But it is *the* integration which also gives hope to all the seemingly futile sufferings of this present world. Without the hope of the Day of the Lord, when God will dwell among us His people and bring peace and harmony to all creation, the existence of so much pain and anguish in our world is the greatest obstacle to belief in a God of love.

Yet, the Resurrection of the crucified Lord, when the Holy Spirit came into the tomb and raised Him on high, points to that Day when everything will be raised up into the presence of God. All the creation with new insight will see a different meaning in all the pains and travails of this world. We shall understand how we have been working with Christ to bring forgiveness and hope to others even in the most adverse and soul-destroying circumstances.

For the creation waits with eager longing for the revealing of the sons of God; for the creation was subjected to futility, not of its own will but by the will of him who subjected it in hope; because the creation itself will be set free from its bondage to decay and obtain the glorious liberty of the children of God (Rom 8:19–21).

All this brings us back to Peter, the dying minister whom I anointed.

Perhaps from a higher faith-level than many of us have yet to reach, he had a far deeper insight and understanding of his death-bed pain and fears than any of us who have yet to walk the valley of the shadow of death.

Perhaps through the prayers, through the anointing, the Holy Spirit came to Peter amid his pain and proper anxieties about dying and leaving his wife and family.

The Holy Spirit baptised him and took him up to that highest faith-level of all in this world and created in him that God-given conviction which *knows* that nothing, absolutely nothing in the whole of creation can ever separate us from God's love.

Perhaps from that highest view of all, he could see *through* that knowledge of God's overwhelming and all-embracing love for him, and understand that even his pain and failing heart were a necessary preliminary stage, but now only a stage, before he entered into his Lord's presence, sound in mind, body and soul.

Jesus said: 'When a woman is in travail she has sorrow, because her hour has come; but when she is delivered of the child, she no longer remembers the anguish, for joy that a child is born into the world' (John 16:21).

I can only aspire to such a faith-level as that, but in my ministry to some Christians on the threshold of death, I have found it to be an experience common to them. At first many struggle with what they have believed and sometimes preached for years, asking themselves in the midst of all their pain whether they really have faith in God.

They are at the edge of their faith.

Then, for some, comes a sort of breakthrough. A light dawns, they might experience a deep warmth, and they are flooded with peace, assurance and love. There is a deep sense that all shall be well.

They know what is to come is far greater than what they are leaving. And knowing that, they seem to embrace everything they are leaving in the conviction that their separation is only temporary.

Perhaps the conviction that the Lord will restore all things is the final baptism we shall receive, enabling us, so often on our death-beds, to see how God's glory and purpose will one day prevail over the whole creation.

But we have no need to wait for our dying moments,

For I *am sure* [wrote he who brushed death so many times] that neither death, nor life, nor angels, nor principalities, nor things present, nor things to come, nor powers, nor height, nor depth, nor anything else in all creation, will be able to separate us from the love of God in Christ Jesus our Lord (Rom. 8, 38–9; my italics).

So no wonder the *risen* Lord commanded his disciples: 'Go into all the world and preach the gospel to the *whole creation*' (Mark 16:15; my italics).

HE IS LORD

Michael Cole

What does it *really* mean to acknowledge that Jesus is Lord? After twenty-five years in the ministry Michael Cole asked himself this question. This book results from his world-wide search for an answer, his personal experience of renewal, and most importantly from the practice of translating his newly acquired insights into spiritual reality in his own life and the life of his parish.

HE IS LORD acknowledges that we need to repent of our failure to make Jesus Lord in our own lives, and looks at the biblical grounds upon which Jesus Christ has the right to be called the Lord and Head of the Church. Michael Cole discusses the implications of this in the areas of worship, leadership, evangelistic and missionary outreach, and in mobilising the gifts and resources of the local congregation, and shows us clearly how the Lordship of Christ applies to all areas of the Christian life.

Michael Cole is Vicar of All Saints, Woodford Wells in North East London and the Chairman of the Council of the South American Missionary Society. He writes the monthly Question and Answer column in Renewal Magazine and is married with five children.

COME, HOLY SPIRIT

David Pytches

Many churches today are seeking and experiencing spiritual renewal. In this practical guide to ministry in the spirit, David Pytches argues that 'the urgent need is to help churches which want to move forward in the Spirit: to show how the gifts can be integrated into ministry, providing checks and balances, and to enable the Body of Christ, under the anointing of the Holy Spirit, to minister God's power in signs and wonders.

'Get this book: it is a goldmine.' **Anglicans for Renewal**

'Will encourage and challenge many.' **Buzz**

'Clearly comes from a great deal of pastoral experience . . . the biblical basis is well developed and questions are honestly faced.' **Church Times**

Bishop David Pytches, formerly Bishop of Chile, Bolivia and Peru, is currently vicar of St Andrew's, Chorleywood in Hertfordshire.

POWER HEALING

John Wimber

The development of a healing ministry is a significant feature of many churches in the eighties. John Wimber tackles this controversial topic by constructing a practical theology of healing. In POWER HEALING he aims to
- present compelling biblical arguments for the practice of a healing ministry, particularly relating to physical healing
- Answer difficult questions such as 'Why isn't everybody healed?'
- provide suggestions for equipping Christians to pray effectively for healing

'. . . a balanced, practical and helpful approach to the subject . . . a must.' **Redemption**

'. . . this book has an awesome potential for good in today's church' **Buzz**

John Wimber is the charismatic founding pastor of the Vineyard Christian Fellowship. His first book, POWER EVANGELISM, has been widely acclaimed.

LISTEN AND LIVE

Colin Urquhart

How can I pray more effectively? How can I receive from God the blessings he promises? LISTEN AND LIVE is Colin Urquhart's response to these questions. Drawing on his own personal and pastoral experience, he provides a way of praying and reading the Bible which has proved both powerful and effective.

Eighty attractive and clearly presented prayer outlines are given, providing an opening sentence, a Bible reading (given in full) and Scriptures for meditation and for praise. A commentary draws out the theme and emphasises how it applies to the individual Christian in practice.

Through using the Bible in prayer, Colin Urquhart asserts, it is possible to receive the love, joy, peace, power, healing and forgiveness of which Jesus speaks, and to direct it towards others.

Colin Urquhart is an Anglican minister, leader of the Bethany Fellowship in Sussex. He has a well-known and widely respected teaching and healing ministry, and is the author of several books including WHEN THE SPIRIT COMES, IN CHRIST JESUS, and RECEIVE YOUR HEALING.